When West Ham *went to the* Dogs

OVER THEY GO - FOUR IN A LINE -
flashes of canine colour as they streak down
the track and over the hurdles. Speed
and grace in every movement. Try
Greyhound Racing one evening.
Meetings every Monday and
Wednesday at 8 p.m.
with eight events
including hurdle
races in every
programme.

ADMISSION: 1/3; 2/-; 2/6; 5/-

When West Ham *went to the* Dogs

Brian Belton

TEMPUS

This book is dedicated to Rosy,
Christian ... and Little Reg.

First published 2002

Published in the United Kingdom by:
Tempus Publishing Ltd
The Mill, Brimscombe Port
Stroud, Gloucestershire GL5 2QG

British Library Cataloguing in Publication Data.
A catalogue record for this book is available from the British Library.

ISBN 0 7524 2722 9

Typesetting and origination by Tempus Publishing.
Printed in Great Britain by Midway Colour Print, Wiltshire.

CONTENTS

ACKNOWLEDGEMENTS

My grandmother used to sell West Ham Greyhound programmes outside the track on race nights. Later, with my dad, she took my brother and me to Custom House to 'see the doggies run'. In time I'd bunk in to watch the meetings, but mostly mix with and observe those people who loved the dogs, punters, trainers, bookmakers and owners. I learnt about dogs, but more importantly this is the place where I started to comprehend what it was that motivated, excited and disappointed people. They were funny, they were good, they were bad tempered, argumentative, loud, shy, obsessive, interesting, talkative, easy going, optimistic and depressed. They were extrovert, cynical, boring, kind and mad. They were liars, cheats, miserable and greedy, nervous, honest and happy. They were wise, stupid, ignorant and intelligent. They were people who inhabited a time, a place and a life. They were human reality in all its forms and they educated me in what it was to live and let live. They showed me how to find generosity in the dark reaches of despair. One day I'll write a book about them, but for now I will write about their world.

What follows was only possible because of the great help munificently given by a number of people. In particular, this history owes its existence to two former track employees Mr Bob Rowe, the one-time racing manager at West Ham, and Mr Tommy Pickett, the head lad at track for most of his racing career. A number of photographs were supplied by Mr Floyd Amphlett of the *Greyhound Star*, a true knight of the track. Another person was inspirational. He is probably the most active historian connected to greyhound racing: Mr Cliff Mettam. These gentlemen all possess the qualities of those who have loved and love the dogs, but they are also good and kind people, hospitable and humane. It is their devotion and affection for their sport, and all those who attended and were involved with West Ham greyhounds that this work is dedicated to.

'GOOYON THE SIX DOG!!!'

FOREWORD

Greyhound racing has always been a big part of my life. When I was small, Dad was involved in bookmaking. He was frequently on the course at Harringay, Wembley, White City (London), Park Royal, Hendon and of course his original home track at West Ham. He was born in East London and as such West Ham, the basis of this, Brian Belton's book, will always have a place in my heart. The stadium had a wonderful atmosphere.

However, I was born not in West Ham but in West Hendon, London, a few hundred yards from Hendon Greyhound Racetrack. Just half a dozen stepping-stones across the Brent Stream, which flowed into Dollis Brook and I was in the owners' and trainers' car park of this stadium, as magic for me and West Ham was for the author of this book. My home was, as such, in easy earshot of the Hendon kennel complex. Little did I know in those first days of 1930s, the very dawn of organised greyhound racing, that this location would greatly influence my life and career. It is hard to communicate how greyhound racing was seen in those days. For kids like me, the enthusiasm generated by greyhound racing was easily equal to that provoked by football and cricket. It dominated our conversation and interest. The names and performances of dogs captivated us and we looked up to the trainers for their intelligence and skill.

After the First World War, Dad furthered his education at the London School of Economics. He was brilliant mathematician and was able to master the percentages and fractions that governed greyhound racing with consummate ease. This made him a very able and gifted Course Clerk. During the early 1940s, dad taught me the 'North Country' totting process that he adopted on course. It proved to be an invaluable method of knowing one's liabilities at any given time and especially useful as my introduction to hedging in later life.

During this period I had the luck of seeing Tricky Mickey, Mickey Fingers as we knew him, in action as a tic-tac at Brighton Racecourse and at Hove Dogs in Neville Road. Fingers was poetry in motion when relaying odds. He was a form of entertainment in himself, able to hold the attention of onlookers and leave youngsters like me spellbound with his dexterity and astuteness. He must have earned his guv'nor countless thousands of pounds, as he was personally able to manipulate the starting prices with a flick of his wrist if he so desired.

After seeing Mickey I used to go home and practice tic-tac in front of the mirror. A useful method as it undoubtedly helps one to receive as well as relay.

It was this that, in 1951, enabled me to gain work with the Magnus firm in the popular enclosure at Hendon Dogs as a floorman tic-tac. Nowadays that hallowed ground is covered by Junction 1 of the M1 Motorway and one of the first mega-size shopping complexes to be built in Britain.

I was to work for the same guv'nor as Mickey at Wembley and Watford (Vicarage Road) Dogs, but before this I was employed by Billy and Alf Mahon and also did some work for Margolis and Ridley. But the introduction of betting shops brought new opportunities. I worked as a boardman for Burns and Downes at Willesden Green. The 'Downes' in the firm's title was Terry Downes, one of the greatest boxers Britain as ever produced. I briefly acted as his chauffeur when he lost his driving licence.

I moved on to the Stan Gilbert Group (turf accountants) and worked at all nineteen of their betting shops. In the early days of these new betting shops, I was a boardman at their Varley Parade shape in Colindale. I wore a brown smock with a duster in the pocket and got smothered in the chalk that was used to show the runners and odds. The racing results and runners came over the Tannoy system thick and fast, including the results from West Ham, down deep in Dad's East End homeland.

During 1959 and the early 1960s I had dogs with Bob Burls at Wembley (I was subsequently granted a private trainer's licence, but that's another story). It was around 1959 that I was formally introduced to Jack Harvey and his wife Angela. Harry (Jack) Harvey was my schoolboy idol. He had already won the Prestigious Greyhound Derby with Davesland in 1934 during his training days at Harringay, when he was living at the famous G.R.A. kennels at Hook Lane in Hertfordshire. Jack later progressed and trained at Wembley on Captain Brice's recommendation. Jack had many successes and in 1955 he had three finalists in the Greyhound Derby, but his Grand National champion, odds on favourite Barrowside, narrowly lost the great race by less than a length. Jack however bounced back in 1959 and won the English, Scottish and Welsh Derbys, thus completing the Triple Crown with the brindle 'Mile Bush Pride'. I was proud to have seen it all and was also at West Ham Stadium the night when Mile Bush Pride trounced the opposition, winning the Cesarewitch as the red hot 2/7 favourite. It was a wonderful night. Mile Bush Pride was to hold the 600-yard track record of 32.65 for many years.

Well, blackboards and chalks were disposed of and new melamine white boards were used with coloured board markers instead of chalk and permanent ink board markers for our s/p headings, which could not be reused by mistake. Now of course coloured television and personalised information screens with all the ante-post prices have superseded boards and the old anker stamping and timing devices. The board man has disappeared into a multicoloured mist of historical chalk dust along, unfortunately, with West Ham's fine old racetrack.

I went on to work at Gilbert's head office in North Finchley dealing with their evening returns. The evenings were especially good when many of their shops had a winning day and the spirits cabinet was opened up by the guv'nors and we all went home 'happy'.

I was floorman tic-tac for Ken Munden at White City London before that stadium, like Custom House a dozen years earlier, closed in the autumn of 1984. Many of my colleagues and the bookmakers there transferred their on-course business interests to Walthamstow, Wimbledon and of course to Wembley Stadium, but that was also to close its doors to greyhound racing on Friday 18 December 1998.

Having got so much from greyhound sport, like Brian Belton I think it is important to preserve and celebrate its history. Anything without a history has no real existence. However, this is not an easy enterprise, because although dog racing is a love of so many, as phenomenon is trapped in the present. My ambition now is to find a secure and permanent museum for the artefacts of the Greyhound Racing Historical Society as a tribute to all the greyhounds, the trainers, the dedicated kennel staff, the owners and personalities associated with the sport of greyhound racing from the early coursing days. Many of them are named in this book and as such I hope that it will help you to realise how much we owe to those who have been closely associated with greyhounds over the centuries. If it hadn't have been for their enthusiasm our sport, and the challenge and enjoyment it gives to so many, would not exist.

Cliff Mettam – Chair of the Greyhound Racing Historical Society

Greyhounds Taking a Hurdle at a Florida Track

Alway's first home... but
never a winner

INTRODUCTION

A day's work

The 1 dog is dressed in the red of fire,
To be away from the crowd is his only desire,
Burning and blazing, the long way round,
Hot in his lonely passion he flames the ground.
When the heat seems extinguished and there's no fear of attack,
That's when the inferno ignites, from the outside of the track.
From '*The Ballad of the West Ham Dogs*'

All sport is frolicsome battle and it demands warrior qualities. In fact the extent to which a sport calls on such skills and instincts, the more it exposes it marshal origins, the more popular it is likely to be. The roots of sporting activity run deep and are entwined in the necessity our far off ancestors had to kill. The echoes of this, the frightening, chaotic elements of sport, are what draw spectators to it. Herein is something more archaic than the simple need for victory, those who have competed in serious sport will know that the 'will to win' is motivated by more fundamental drives that have their origins in ancient hunger and primitive needs to pursue or escape.

When we watch greyhounds shooting out of the traps we see creatures riding their instincts to catch and kill as they seek to run down an artificial hare. Track racing evolved from coursing and that 'sport' developed out of the need for food. This hits something at the core of our being and vibrates the strings of our biological heritage.

If you should see a wolf chase another creature as its food, you perceive a controlled panic fired by desperation. When one views a hound, not particularly in need of sustenance, chase a smaller creature with every intention of killing it, what you are observing is a clash between fear and desire. To be one of hundreds or thousands watching a greyhound in pursuit of a hare that can't be caught, the excitement of the punter, the owner and the trainer has its source in need. The phantom of the kill is still present. The essence of the sport is that heady, primeval mixture of chaos and fear. It is this that charms people to involve themselves with greyhounds.

This is to not say that a night out at the dogs is motivated by a kind of blood lust, although anyone who has been to a greyhound meeting will have heard frustrated punters vent their spleen; 'Fall over yer bastard' and 'Break the fucker's back' are a couple of recent cries I have come across and have heard variations of over the years. I picked up a very original order just before writing this book: 'Get back under the table you shit-coloured nonce'. The people who articulated these 'instructions' are unlikely to have actually meant them. The words give expression to feelings; they are not prescriptions for action or notifications of intention. The words encapsulate expressions of desperation, dashed hopes and pain, but they are said in the context of the frivolity that is sport. These words do not carry harm in this environment premised on the yearnings fired by imagination. It is the same in other sports; for instance, at a Celtic v. Rangers match you might hear the green-clad supporters singing of 'wading through Protestant blood', but that doesn't mean that is what they want to do. It is provocative, but that is all that it is as long as it is part of a frivolous sporting context. Those who wish to rid sport of such provocation do not understand sport or simply do not want sport to exist in society. In the sporting situation of greyhound racing the fact is that we spill money rather than blood and give time and effort in training and sorting form rather than in tracking, but we are there, at West Ham, Walthamstow, Wimbledon or wherever, fulfilling a definite and very old psychophysical drive.

In a way this book is a history of the playing out of this drive within the milieu of West Ham greyhound racing that took place at the massive East End arena sometimes known as Custom House Stadium and at others called West Ham Stadium. Dog racing meetings were held at this venue from the earliest days of the sport in Britain until the start of the 1970s, when the site of this noble amphitheatre was sold to developers.

However, how does one start to write such a history? Over the near half century that West Ham hosted greyhound sport, there were something like 7,500 meetings. That's about 75,000 races and 450,000 runners. The number of dogs that ran at West Ham exceeded 5,000. But how can one understand what West Ham was unless it is placed in the world of which it was a part? To write the story of a greyhound track without elaborating its historical context and how it fitted in with the world of dog racing is about as wise as organizing a greyhound meeting but neglecting to arrange for the use of a track and a stadium.

The pages that follow will tell the story of the development of greyhound sport from a 'West Ham' perspective, as West Ham greyhound racing grew as part of and alongside the sport of which it was a representative part. It will,

Noble Racing Hounds

through West Ham's record holders and Classic winners, show how greyhound racing generated and grew in its East End, national and international incarnations. But, the main path I have chosen to explore and illuminate the meaning, function and fact of West Ham greyhound racing is its cockney Classic, the Cesarewitch. This definite reference point gives some orientation in time and a sense of the place that West Ham occupied in the expansion and demise of greyhound sport. The Cesarewitch also helps demonstrate West Ham's role in a world and a culture based upon competition and expressed through breeding, training and gambling.

So, let's go to the dogs. Get there for the first race, so we can see how the form is going, how the track is shaping. It was always worth the effort. The dogs at West Ham were another world; a world apart, a place often used to escape, but it was never escapism — it was always too real for that. But while you're there it's hard to think of anything else.

There's fifty years of racing ahead. Magicians like Biss and Appleton have brought some wonderful dogs that will run for us – there's Mick and Jewel, the Queen and the Prince and many, many more. Get a good place to watch from, it's gonna be packed...They're going in the traps!

That bitch in the blue,
Runs from trap 2,
In her cold attire,
She does aspire,
To be the first over the line,
In a track record time.

Chilly Queen of azure,
She is frosty and pure

Demure in rime,
She is awesome and fine.
With an icy stare,
She pursues the hare,
Her backers she'll please,
As her combatants freeze,
And the victory she'll deliver,
Bequeathing only defeat's harsh shiver.

From *'The Ballad of the West Ham Dogs'*

1
SOLOMON'S DOGS

The Greyhound

I have myself bred up a hound whose eyes are the greyest of grey; a swift, hard-working soft-footed dog; in his prime a match at any time for four hares. He is moreover most gentle and kindly affectioned. Never before had any dog such regard for myself and friend and fellow sportsman, Megillus . . . He is the constant companion of whichever of us may be sick; and if he has not seen either us for but a short time, he jumps up repeatedly by way of salutation, barking with joy as a greeting to us . . .

Thus wrote Flavius Arrianus. Arrian, as the writer is better known, was born in Nicomedia in Asia Minor and became a citizen of Athens. Later, through his consular work, he became a Roman citizen and advanced to senatorial dignities. Familiar with the greyhound breed from his youth, he wrote the earliest known treatise on the greyhound (the *cynegeticus*), of which the above is part. It was written in the second century AD, when Hadrian was Emperor, but it was not discovered until the late eighteenth century, in the Vatican archives. It was translated by 'A Graduate of Medicine' in 1831 and shows Arrian as a most humane man and a great lover of greyhounds. However, humanity's love for this breed seems to go back to times even before Arrian.

They're in the traps

The stands are packed full of expectant and anxious spectators. The six Greyhound Derby finalists, muscles rippling lazily under their lightweight jackets, complete their parade with the green of the centre track in the background. The multi-coloured board flashes the latest betting figures that occupy the attention of the stadium's East End punters. The bookmakers

Hammerin' round

gathered round the home straight, beneath the main stand, shout the last-minute odds, which are frantically signaled across the stadium by white-gloved tic-tac men. Kennel lads in bowler hats carefully lodge their canine charges in the starting boxes. A starting bell rings out and the stadium lights dim. The racetrack becomes an illuminated oval ribbon under blazing overhead lamps. The audience of 35,000 is silenced for what seems like an eternal second, as the electronic hare, heard before it is seen, wobbles and whirls to a start. As this perennial fugitive, 'Harry' at West Ham, 'Swifty' in Florida, picks up speed, the crowd releases the famous Cesarewitch roar, which mounts to an eruption of noise as the hare tears past the starting box. Up spring the traps with an instant 'thwack' and a blurring streak of six champion greyhounds fly free in hot pursuit of their quarry. For the winner there will be fame and for its owner there will be fortune. The chase through these incident-packed bends and straights lasts not much more than 30 seconds, and another Classic event in British greyhound racing is over for another year. The winner, who may have cost a working man's weekly wage as a pup, or the equivalent of half a year's earnings for the average West Ham Stadium spectator as a grown dog, is led to the presentation dais, tail wagging, to receive the gold and blue jacket of honour. A cup and cheques are presented to owner and trainer.

To greyhound racing enthusiasts across the planet and over time, this scene will be familiar. A description of the American Derby at Taunton, in the United States, or the National Greyhound Sprint Championship in Sydney, Australia would have been little different. The essential elements would also be found in Ireland, Spain, the Canary Islands, New Zealand, Indonesia, Macao (China), Italy, Norway, Sweden, Denmark, Germany, Finland, the Netherlands and Switzerland, although betting is not permitted in some of these countries.

This pattern, this set of traditions, arises out of the history of racing greyhounds on an oval track, which extends back in time less than one hundred years, but it is also the product of the intimate relationship between humanity and greyhound ancestry that can be traced back several thousands of years. It is mentioned in the Bible and the breed has been prized by a number of civilizations and peoples as a hunting dog. What we call 'the greyhound' is a dog that has been shaped and is still being shaped by human needs and desires. This might seem manipulative, but this interaction has been of mutual benefit to both canine and human kind.

The greyhound is a 'lively breed'. Its continued relevance and role in society stands in stark contrast to other types of dog that have either disappeared or lost their place as active creatures, able to give full reign to their instincts and unique gifts. The greyhound has not become a cosseted creature, the type that inhabits the domestic dens of modern urban society. It has been able to avoid much of the indignity of character repression that many of the fighters and hunters of old have been subject to at the behest of human whim. The greyhound is not the colonised animal, taught to beg and roll over. It may run after a hare, but it might be less likely to bring it back. The greyhound still seeks out a prey and runs in packs in pursuit of the same. The dog is lauded for the capabilities bestowed upon it by nature and its fame is derived from its might, its courage and intelligence. As such, the greyhound, like few other breeds, has, in its relationship with humanity, held on to its distinction and pride, in that it has retained its essential personality. Anyone who has seen a greyhound race will recognise this: its hunger for the chase before the hare has come into its sight and its obvious pleasure in its own performance when the race has been run. This dignity that arises out of the greyhound's common interests with human beings has given the breed an honoured place in society and history.

Race day

The greyhound, alongside its cousins the Persian saluki, the Afghan hound and the borzoi of the Russian Steppes, has its origins in the desert of southern Arabia. These animals would have found their way to Egypt by way of the incense trade, as part of the caravans that criss-crossed this part of the world, serving the ancient civilisations that lived and thrived there. The Necropolis at Wl-Ourna, close to Thebes on the Nile, contains murals that include hounds with leg and ear featherings similar to those associated with the saluki. The greyhound is imprinted on the palm of the ostrich feathers found in Tutankhamun's tomb. The dog depicted is strikingly reminiscent of those that would have struck out of the traps at West Ham, and their kith and kin that race on the modern race tracks of the twenty-first century.

In the Old Testament the greyhound is one of Solomon's 'four things which are most comely in going'. As such, it would be likely that the Queen of Sheba took a number of her finest animals with her when she visited Solomon in Jerusalem around 1000 BC. There is a West Country legend that a pair of these, having been gifted to Solomon, were brought to England, to Tintagel in Cornwall, and exchanged for a shipload of the precious tin that was mined there. The tale goes on that when the boy Jesus was brought to the same part of the world a millennium later, accompanying his trading uncle, Joseph of Arimathea, he saw some of the descendants of Solomon's dogs being coursed. The young carpenter's son felt pity for the hare, who didn't seem to have a chance against the sharp-eyed, lightning fast hounds, but he was also sorry for one of the dogs, who having failed to win for its master was being beaten violently. It is at this mythical point that the greyhound breed's sense of smell was curtailed, but the animal was compensated with an affable personality and the ability to provoke human affection.

As the hound reached the cooler, more northerly parts of Persia it grew a thicker coat to become the Persian wolfhound. It joined forces with human hunters to fight off the threat of wolves and bears, starting to create the empathy, solidarity and sense of teamwork that developed to make co-operative, symbiotic activity between the species possible.

As the breed made its way further north, to the mountainous regions of Afghanistan, its coat became more substantial. The dog evolved into the Afghan hound. The breed also became taller, a result of needing to see over the rocky ground of its habitat. So, when this 'new, improved' mountain dweller reached the Crimea, it was no longer the saluki of southern Arabia. Its increased height and dense coat now made it a match for cold winters. This was the elegant borzoi: muscular but diaphanous dogs, able to reach high speeds quickly. Thus they had the power to reach their prey before it had the time to escape. This was a necessity, as they hunted by sight, not, like most other hounds, by scent. This characteristic, that required the hound to develop stealth and a silent approach, has led to a relatively quiet dog. The breed rarely barks; noise gives away position.

Making its way from the Middle and Near East the hound came to Greece. Alexander the Great, who had annexed Syria to Greece early on in his career of

GREYHOUND RACING

every

MON. & WED. during OCTOBER

OPEN RACE EVERY WEDNESDAY

The best racing in perfect comfort between England's fastest greyhounds.

Win, Place & Forecast Totalisators : large car parks ; numerous refreshment bars ; easy of access from all parts.

Admission : 1/6, 2/3, 3/-, 5/6   *(including race card)*

WEST HAM STADIUM

Under the Rules of the National Greyhound Racing Club.

GREYHOUND RACING

The National Sport of Thousands.

West Ham Stadium provides London's best racing under ideal conditions. Clean, healthy, thrilling sport every Monday and Wednesday at 8 p.m. Eight races with full Totalisator facilities in every enclosure.

MONDAY NEXT :
NORTH COTSWOLD STAKES
— 600 yards flat —

Admission :   1/3 ;   2/- ;   2/6 ;   5/-.

conquest, may have introduced it. It was probably in Syria that the smooth-haired greyhound originated – the Greek nobility had used the dog for hunting some time before they extended their influence into Syria. It is in this context and time that the cult of Diana appeared, which itself was derived from older traditions of hunting goddesses. The association of greyhounds with hunting traditions and rites meant that the dog renewed its Egyptian connections with the supernatural but also its relationship with the procurement of sustenance, sport and enjoyment. It had become an important possession for practical, social and spiritual reasons.

It was this role that took the greyhound to Italy and eventually, with the Roman colonisers, to Britain, where the locals were quick to take the dog to their hearts. An illuminated manuscript of the ninth century AD, which can now be found in the British Museum, shows a Saxon chieftain and his huntsmen coursing with greyhounds, which can be seen to be similar to the racing dogs that pitched and ran at Custom House up to the last third of the twentieth century.

A law of Canute, dated 1016, deemed that 'None but a gentleman' was allowed to keep a greyhound, which was held to be above all other breeds, to be kept only by those of royal descent. An old Welsh proverb had it that, 'You can tell a gentleman by his greyhound and his hawk'. But they were not always used for the most gentlemanly purposes. Following William the Bastard's victory at Hastings, the Norman Barons who occupied the land just to the east of London town would use greyhounds to chase poachers on the fringes of the great greenwood that was Epping Forest. They were deployed not as trackers but as a kind of instant response to perpetrators that were within sight. Not a few poor local peasants looking to supplement their family's lowly diet with a hare or a rabbit were literally torn to pieces and eaten alive by packs of Norman hounds. Such was the hatred generated by this practice that it was rumoured that it was the Conqueror himself who ordered his henchmen to desist from the practice, deeming that it was a task below his noble dogs.

At the time of the crusades King John would accept greyhounds in lieu of taxes. It is recorded that during his reign William de Brecosa was given three castles in Monmouthshire in return for ten greyhounds and several other dogs, this included a huge black dog, Postle, who de Brecosa had picked up on his way back from the Holy Land. John Engayne was given the Manor of Upminster for 'rearing and keeping greyhounds' for King John collected in this way and by other means. Engayne was to take charge of the legendary Postle, who, as the story goes,

> . . . ran faster than the hind . . . and was . . . the most knowledgeable of dogges . . . who was able . . . to see a hare in hide from near a mile off . . . and . . . twas the most vigorous of his kind, but doting on his master's command . . .

Postle was involved in many a hunting expedition to Epping Forest and became renowned for his exploits. When he died, at the reputed age of sixteen years, much of western Essex, which would have included the area where West Ham Stadium would one day stand, went into mourning. To the last he had been a hunter, having died of 'fragile heart' when, 'arising from slumber at his master's gate' he attempted to pursue a passing stoat.

The wife of Robert the Bruce of Scotland, when a prisoner of Edward I, was allowed to keep 'three women servants and three greyhounds'. This trio of hefty animals, collectively known as the sisters, and believed to be of:

> Postle's pedigree, were a great comfort to her and, it was fabled, allowed the Bruce some rest knowing that his wife at least had the dogs they both loved to keep her company in captivity.

From all of this one can tell that the greyhound in England was a dog with aristocratic connections. Edward III, and later Charles II, had the greyhound incorporated into their seals. However, perhaps more significantly, again, it can be seen that the greyhound has always affected people with a strange mixture of the carnal spirit, embodied in the hunt, and sensibility and emotional attachment generally associated with the familial bond.

What's in a name?

In literature Chaucer, who lived during the reign of Edward III, was the first to use the word 'greihound', spelt almost as it is today, in *The Canterbury Tales*: 'Greihounds he had as swift as fowl of flight'.

From then on the greyhound pops up occasionally, sometimes in the writings of the most unlikely of scribes. In 1481 Dame Juliana Berners, prioress of the nunnery of Sopwell, was the first to set down the 'Points of a good greyhound' in her famous *Booke of St Albans*, printed by Wynkin de Worde, Caxton's most famous assistant. It is fascinating because the 'points' hold good to this day. A greyhound, said the prioress, should have:

> A head lyke a snake,
> A neck lyke a drake,
> The feet of a cat
> A tail lyke a rat.
> A back lyke a beam,
> The sides of a bream.

Maybe a more contemporary analysis might include 'the brain of a tank commander'.

Shakespeare, in *Henry V*, shows his familiarity with hare coursing in the king's famous speech to his troops before Harfleur:

I see you stand like greyhounds in the slips,
Straining upon the leash. The game's afoot;
Follow your spirit; and upon this charge,
Cry – God for Harry! England! And St George!

In many of his plays which have rural settings, Shakespeare mentions the greyhound and coursing, as for instance in *The Merry Wives of Windsor*, in which Master Slender says to Page: 'How does your fallow greyhound? I heard say he was outrun on Cotsall.' [Cotswold]

The name 'greyhound' is likely to have been bestowed on it in the light of the dog's hunting credentials: the Icelandic greyhundr, grey meaning dog, hundr meaning hunter. The popular belief that the hound was given its name as an elusion to its colour seems a little simplistic as greyhounds have come in a variety of hues, but the eyes of many hounds were soft grey, as Arrian (see the top of this chapter) pointed out, and the pre-modern breed often had a soft grey coat.

Several other explanations have been put forward as to the derivation of the name 'greyhound'. Dr Caius, co-founder of Gonville and Caius College, Cambridge, believed the name was derived from the Anglo-Saxon gre or grieg meaning 'first in rank' of hounds. Later, gre became gradus, meaning 'first grade' or 'most important'. In a letter to the German naturalist Conrad Gesner, Dr Caius wrote that the hound's moniker seemed to suggest that it was, 'amongst alle doggs this was the most principalle, occupying the highest place'. If ever you're in Cambridge, keep an eye open for depictions of greyhounds on the decorations of the older colleges.

Others believe the dog's name to be derived from 'gaze', alluding to the dog's keen sight when out hunting. All of these ideas have some credence and it is probable that no single one of them is correct – in fact the designation 'greyhound' has been adopted and ascribed on the collective impact of all these explanations and others lost in antiquity.

Hair and the hare

There were two distinct types of greyhound in Britain, the long-haired and the short-haired. The Elizabethan writer Gervase Markham wrote that the long-haired 'are held most proper for the vermin and wild beasts . . . but not the other, which are more smooth and delicately proportioned and are best for pleasure…'

This illustrates that by the first Elizabethan period the smooth-haired greyhound was considered too cultured to be hunting creatures like the wolf, wild boar or deer that inhabited the 'green wood' of old Albion. In his *Miscellanies*, Tichel mentions both types of dogs. He claimed that the long-haired, which he called the gage-hound, was used for stalking deer, whilst the shorter-haired greyhound was deployed in hare coursing:

> See'st thou the gagehound, how with glance severe
> From the close herd, he marks the destined deer;
> How every nerve the greyhound's stretch displays
> The hare, preventing in her airy maze . . .

As might be gathered from above, in Britain it seems that the smooth-haired hound was held in higher esteem, but it was Lord Orford who was to become the first human to systematically attempt to develop the breed. In the eighteenth century he crossed the smooth-haired strain with a bulldog. For the first time the now familiar brindle coat appeared, a blend of shades of brown, grey and black emerging as asymmetrical stripes and markings. Before Orford's intervention greyhounds had, in the main, been black, white or a mixture of the two. There are now also blue and fawn animals, but greyhounds are not and have never been essentially grey animals, in colour or character.

The bulldog breed

Orford continued crossing bulldogs with greyhounds for seven generations. The effect was a more courageous and, in terms of hunting focus, aggressive dog, but the subsequent animal also had improved stamina. These qualities did much to promote and popularise the short, silky-coated dog we now know so well. Orford produced what was described at the time as 'the best greyhound ever known'. This is the racing animal that ran at West Ham: the one to six dogs of the modern era.

Many of Orford's contemporaries had reservations about his ideas connected with dog breeding. However, his methods were vindicated by one of the early champions coming from the 'bulldog breed'. King Cob was the first dog whose services at stud were available to bitches belonging to the public. From King Cob's breeding the great Master M'Grath was produced. He won the Waterloo Cup, the world championship of coursing, on three occasions, 1868, 1869 and 1871. But it was Orford's bitch Czarina who was to produce the finest coursing stock the world had ever known. Her first litter didn't arrive until she was thirteen years old, but it included Claret, the dog that would later become the sire of the celebrated Snowball.

Major Topham of the Malton Club in Yorkshire owned Snowball. The dog was to win four major trophies and 30 courses before being retired to stud. The modern track greyhound is the progeny of Claret and Snowball and the latter was to figure in the pedigree of a whole lineage of famous greyhounds of the early period, including Fly, which through Oliver Twist, who was narrowly beaten in a Waterloo Cup final, appeared in the ancestry of the brood bitch Fudge. Her son Judge won the Waterloo Cup in 1855 and in turn sired subsequent winners in Maid of the Mill (1860) and Chloe (1863). In fact, all of Judge's daughters were outstanding coursing animals and later quality dams. The breeding world recognises that the whole structure of modern greyhound breeding was built upon the bitches sired by Judge, the grandson of Snowball, who was himself the grandson of Lord Orford's bitch Czarina.

Coursing – before the traps

All this work on developing sporting greyhounds was not expended to simply produce 'racing' dogs. What Orford and his ilk were looking to produce were top quality coursing animals, hunters more than runners. There are few more controversial or more exciting distractions for the enthusiast of canine hunting sport than coursing for hares. The sheer speed and precision of the course, together with the physical, emotional and technical perfection of the dogs make it a thrilling pursuit for owners and followers. Yet the violent death of the prey and the large number of hares that die in a day's coursing make it a subject of revulsion to others, to the extent that reforms have become a matter that has taken a huge amount of parliamentary time and energy over recent years.

A course is, in its simplest terms, a race between two specially bred greyhounds to catch a hare that has been driven into a space by a line of beaters so that it must run past the greyhounds. As the hare dashes past the dogs they will see it and attempt to chase it, but they are held back until the hare has cleared the hounds by approximately 30-50 metres, then the two hunters are slipped simultaneously by the slipper, the person who holds them on a leash until the appropriate moment. The dogs then compete to catch the hare.

Points are awarded by the judges mounted on horseback (in order that they can see exactly what happens) for the speed of the individual dogs, for turning the hare at right-angles as it runs, for a wrench (turning it at less than a right-angle), for tipping the hare off its feet, and for the final kill. It may be true that a greyhound kills the hare very quickly by itself, but if both the dogs involved in the contest reach the hare at precisely or around the same time, the course may end in a live tug-of-war between the dogs, with the hare screeching between the jaws of the rivals.

A good coursing greyhound is streamlined and agile. The head is wide, tapering to a long nose. The chest is very deep, with a wide ribcage to facilitate a strong heart and big lungs. The neck should be relatively long and muscular to enable the dog to catch the hare without losing its stride. The hind legs, which are the main means of the animal's propulsion, must be extremely powerful. The forelegs should be firm and long to match the stride of the hind legs and hold the body steady between strides.

Coursing, which is a kind of formalised hunt, has been a popular, organised pastime (many would argue against it being called a sport) for many hundreds of years. One story as to why the Isle of Dogs, not too far from where West Ham Greyhound track would one day stand, was so called because King Edward III is believed to have kept his coursing greyhounds there. The first set of rules for coursing were formulated in Britain in the 1500s and in 1836 the proprietor of the Waterloo Hotel in Liverpool founded the Waterloo Cup, a trophy that is

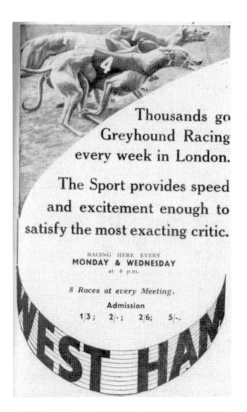

Thousands go
Greyhound Racing
every week in London.

The Sport provides speed
and excitement enough to
satisfy the most exacting critic.

RACING HERE EVERY
MONDAY & WEDNESDAY
at 8 p.m.

8 Races at every Meeting.

Admission
1/3 ;   2/- ;   2/6 ;   5/-.

TOMORROW

|

SECOND ROUND
MAY STAKES
400 yds. Flat

Semi-Finals   Monday Next
Final - Wednesday (May 13th)

+++++++

All the fastest sprinters
in   London   Competing

+++++++

8 Races   *8 p.m.*

Admission
1/3 ;   2/- ;   2/6 ;   5/-.

competed for in February of each year. It became the Classic event in the coursing calendar. In England the coursing season started in September and continued through to March. Whilst greyhounds were running at Custom House, from November onwards there was a course on most days at one of the 23 clubs.

The United States also stage their version of the Waterloo Cup annually. Coursing in America is controlled by the National Coursing Association of America, which is based in Abilene in Kansas. In addition to the Waterloo Cup, other major events have included the American Field Cup and the Columbus Cup.

Barbarism in the countryside

The ongoing debate about, and the threat of, legal restrictions may curtail officially organised legal live coursing in Britain, but this does not mean an end of such activity. An article in *The Observer* (16 December 2001) reflected a new 'cultural' response to the seeming demise of controlled coursing. Under the headline, 'Barbarism in the countryside: Britain's illegal blood sport boom', Anthony Barnett reported:

> They meet every Sunday in gangs of up to 40, assembling at secret rural locations across Britain. Some of the men are armed with shotguns; some wear balaclavas. Many drive off-road vehicles and have travelled hundreds of miles for the illegal meet, which has been arranged over mobile phones. Their dogs, mostly lurchers, bark.
>
> This is illegal hare coursing, a craze that is being dubbed 'the new dog fighting'. More than a dozen such events have taken place recently. The aim is simple: to bet on how many hares your dog can kill.
>
> Once on a farm, the gang release their dogs, which race through crops or livestock searching for their prey, the brown hare. If it is their dog that has killed the hare, they stand to make a lot of money.
>
> Tomorrow, legal hare coursing and fox-hunting resume after a 10-month ban on blood sports since the outbreak of foot and mouth disease.
>
> But illegal coursing is still big business. Up to £20,000 can change hands in one day. The best dogs can win their owners more than £40,000.
>
> The craze presents enormous problems for farmers, many of whom are still recovering from the effects of foot and mouth. The gangs wreck crops, harm livestock and damage property. They try to intimidate farmers who take action against them.
>
> In the past few months, meetings have happened in Sussex, Oxfordshire, Cambridgeshire, Lincolnshire, Essex, Humberside and East Anglia. In Kent, more than 25 farms have reported damage from coursing. One farmer in Kent said: 'I was threatened and warned that they knew which car my wife drove. Other farmers who have told police have found their barns alight.

They drove across my fields, ruining my crops and scaring my livestock.' Robert Jackson, MP for Wantage in Oxfordshire, which has had many problems with illegal hare coursing, has raised the issue in the Commons.

'For landowners it is a problem and farmers have been threatened', he said. 'Hare coursing with trespass has become a favourite weekend occupation for substantial numbers of rough urban dwellers, who will drive hundreds of miles for a days' "sport"'.

Who cares about hares?

Such are the dangers of an authoritarian approach to any cultural pastime or tradition. The official/legislative banning leads to the usual litigious outcome; all external/overt control of the offending activity and the potential for censorship of the same is lost and power is handed to the mob. Much police time will be spent looking to control such atrocities as detailed above, but whilst there is a will and motivation, like cock- and dogfighting, it will not be stamped out, no matter how much any one relatively small group of people want this.

Coursing involves cold-blooded killing. The death of the hare is not always swift; indeed, it can be vile carnage. The less well organised an event the more the latter is likely, so banning managed coursing is likely to promote animal suffering rather and diminish the same. However, should society, by keeping coursing legal, condone the cruelty involved? But this question provokes other questions. Does the banning of blood sports take cruelty out of life? Would the world be a better place without cruelty or suffering? Is this possible anyway? Is what hounds do to hares cruel, bearing in mind that a hare can eat its own young? Even if we say it is, can human beings legislate against it?

As a society we have perhaps simply not learned to live with ourselves. Maybe we need to accept and/or manage some of the instincts, drives, passions or even needs that exist, possibly not in all of us, but certainly in some of us. Even the most tolerant will only accept that which is tolerable; after that even the most liberal will become intolerant and look to the force of law, or even physical attack, to dictate behaviour rather than pursue rational argument and informed persuasion. A minority will be supported as long as it does not offend the sensibilities and values of those doing the supporting; as soon as these are breached, support for that minority is restricted or withdrawn. This is the most blatant form of patronisation and a species of covert control. The cynic would be understood if they pointed out the hypocrisy of the seemingly tolerant, liberal, the likes of the vocal adherents of the abolition of coursing. Perhaps the knowledge of what coursing is really like would do more for its demise than the use of draconian law.

This is what happens – two hounds yowl and drool as they are held at the neck until the hare has been released from its box or beaten from the undergrowth. She (the hare is always referred to as 'she') runs about 70 or 80 yards ahead of the dogs. Some of the smallish crowd of country gentlefolk are baying in time for the slaughter; she is startled by this and moves in a straight line. The hunters are slipped from their hang rope leash and they hurtle towards their quarry and she begins to sense that speed alone will not save her and she calls on her natural weapons of lissomness to confuse her pursuers. A miasma of checking, swerving, scuffling and swivelling ensues. Desperation, dread, fear, desire are prised into stark reality, made material as the spirit of instinct conjures up the bloody nature gods that engulf the brain – this is a high, a drug like trip, wherein the spectator is given a glimpse of the deep inners of their own animal being. That small green worm, the hypothalamus, which sits at the reptilian core of the fluffy pink cauliflower in our heads, is stimulated.

The dogs are screaming in urgent wants. The hare stands out, she is made more real by the context, her panic is evident, she scampers madly but looks static, trapped in the event. Her whole body is forced to perform a chain of physical feats that would seem beyond her, her pounding limbs bang out a frenzied warning that transfers through the ground and can be felt by spectators up through their legs and into their stomachs. As the small creature tires she begins to stumble, her twists and checks become laboured, more sluggish, the will is being drained as she is nipped and caught momentarily by the hounds. She weakens as the taste of her blood causes the dogs to dig even deeper into their carnal reserves. Their want of her flesh is tangible.

The hare now dances the dance of death, a ridiculous, hopeless, gangling tap routine, in equilibrium between her two torturers who suddenly engulf this pitiful comedian. They tug and pull the clown between them, her eyes bulge from her head, yearning meaninglessly, in sublime terror, towards the small, still chanting huddle of 'spectators'. The living Christmas cracker screeches its last primeval note into the blind, deaf, uncaring, gun-metal grey sky.

Half-an-hour later all that is left of the carnage are the echoes in the mind, that remain, like unremitting scars, forever, and a few streaks of hare blood on the chilly, stiff grass.

Blood sports are an acceptance of cruelty, no different from other acts of violence, despite their subterfuge of respectability. In the place of the humane personal and emotional identification humans can have with other forms of life, they set up a masquerade of gentility that has all the accoutrements of style, 'class' and fashion to bolster it. However, what is being camouflaged is a barbarity, a circus of blood lust. Should we ban it? Why do we need to? Perhaps we might better address the forces in society or the psyche that motivate the official or unofficial course. Until we do that, no matter what statutes are added to the dusty realms of law, it or its progeny will continue.

O.P. Smith and the mechanical hare

The germ of greyhound racing as a sport was planted in England, but bore fruit elsewhere. The British seem to have a national genius for invention or

'Harry' the hare

discovery, though frequently they have failed to make a practical use of ideas that have brought prosperity to others. Many believe that the first greyhound racing meeting took place in a field near the Welsh Harp, Hendon Way, North London in 1876. It was recorded that the 'hare' was dragged along by a rope attached to a windlass worked by band. As such it was the first chronicled instance of a dummy hare being used to entice the greyhounds to race. The following account came from *The Times* of 11 September 1876, under the title 'Coursing by Proxy'.

> To see a pack of greyhounds in pursuit of their prey, it will not in future be necessary to wait for the close of the year, or to repair to some remote moorland country, and there to bide one's time in cold and damp weather for the chance of obtaining a momentary glimpse of the hounds in full chase. Thanks to an ingenious mechanism, it will soon be possible to see this any day in the year, and within less than an hour's journey from the heart of London. In a field near the Welsh Harp, at Hendon, a course has, in fact, been already laid off for hunting an 'artificial hare'.
>
> For a distance of 400 yards in a straight line, a rail has been laid down in the grass. It is traversed through its whole length by a groove, in which runs an apparatus like a skate on wheels. On this sort of shuttle is mounted the 'artificial hare'. It is made to travel along the ground at any required pace, and so naturally to resemble the living animal that it is eagerly pursued by greyhounds. On Saturday afternoon, at half-past three o'clock, a trial was made of the new mechanical arrangement. A considerable number of persons were present.
>
> Although within a short distance of the Welsh Harp, the field is hid from neighbouring houses by a railway embankment, and is quite secluded. The whole scene was that presented by a racecourse. The rail over which the sham hare runs is hid in the grass, and the windlass by which the apparatus is moved does not catch the eye of the spectator. When the hour came all that was seen was the 'artificial hare' bounding out, quite naturally, like the

real animal, from its bag, and followed at once by the hounds, like so many kittens after a cork. It was amusing to watch the eager greyhounds in their headlong race, striving in vain with all their might to overtake the phantom hare, which a touch of the windlass could send spinning like a shadow away out of their reach.

The new sport is undoubtedly an exciting and interesting one. It is, perhaps, entitled to the commendation bestowed upon it by the promoters. 'It is,' they say, 'well worthy of the attention of the opponents of sports involving cruelty to animals, as it will afford an innocent recreation to all, without the faintest shadow of the reproach of cruelty attaching to it.' As a minor recommendation, we are told that it supplies a means of training greyhounds, but its usefulness in this respect is to be proved. In the course of recent trials of the apparatus, it is stated that the hounds succeeded more than once in catching the hare, which they tore into shreds with destructive fury. Whether this is to become a part of future performances we do not know.

It is appropriate that another letter from *The Times* of 30 June 1927 should be given as an addendum to the above. Mr Philip E. Noble, Jesmond Dene House, Newcastle-on-Tyne, wrote:

The statement is made in the article in your issue of June 25th that Mistley can claim to have won the first greyhound race after the mechanical hare ever held in this country. Mr. William Hedley-Dent, of Shortflatt, the son of Mr. Edward Dent (the breeder and trainer of Fullerton), furnished me with the following particulars with regard to his father's first success with greyhounds. Mr. Edward Dent won the Kingsbury Stakes of the mechanical hare meeting held at the Welsh Harp, Hendon, October 14, 1876. The name of the greyhound was Charming Nell, by Bacchanal out of Canonbie. With regard to this bitch his diary reads: 'Bought Charming Nell at Aldridge's for 10s. 6d. Coomassie sold to Caffley same sale for 10s. 6d.' (won two Waterloo Cups).

It appears that the reporter of 1876 was not a 'sporting man' or he would have avoided speaking of a 'pack of greyhounds'. Nor would he have used some of the other terms that sound strange to anyone concerned with coursing. For all this, the venture was not a success for a number of reasons, but probably the biggest drawback was the use of a straight course, which meant that the fastest dog invariably won.

The recognized founder of modern greyhound racing was Owen Patrick Smith, an Oklahoma sportsman. In 1907 he had promoted a coursing meeting in Salt Lake City and it had given him the idea of holding a meeting in a confined space with the dogs chasing a dummy hare. However, he had to modify his concept in response to the legal restrictions on coursing in the USA at the time, where it was against the law to hold coursing meetings within prescribed boundaries of a given area. As such he began to develop the notion of racing greyhounds in the pursuit of an artificial quarry. Not long after this, whilst in Tucson, Arizona, he met an Irishman by the name of Tom Keen. These two enthusiasts built a mechanical hare and put it to the test in a field outside New Orleans, but without success. Smith had faith in his vision, however, for the next few years he worked hard on his project, attempting to develop an artificial lure suitable for an oval or circular track. As early as 1912 he applied for a patent for a dummy hare.

In 1919 Smith's tenacity was rewarded when the first sizeable meeting deploying his invention took place on a crude track he had built in Emeryville, California. With the assistance of a certain George Sawyer, the track was a success and each week more people were converted to the racing. A year later a track was opened in Tulsa. But Smith was now down to his last dollar after spending more than ten years and a small fortune on his dream. However, Americans wishing to forget the experience of the First World War were looking for excitement and the sport took off in Tulsa. Within a few months another facility was built at Hialeah, Florida, a state that would be at the forefront of the promotion of greyhound racing in the USA.

A year or two before the USA wholeheartedly embraced greyhound racing some Americans crossed the Atlantic, acting on behalf of a company in California, and tried to obtain the support of prominent British sportsmen for the opening tracks in England. But the greyhound sport that was embodied in coursing with its Elizabethan roots, its rules, codes and traditions that had hardly changed down the ages was not ready for progress. Centuries of convention and an accompanying snobbery could not be lightly disregarded. Greyhound racing was something of anathema to this cartel, being the apotheosis of speed, without giving the dogs the opportunity of exhibiting the other forms of cleverness (and viciousness) required on the coursing field. Britain was just not ready for new-world innovation within a solidly old world sport. The Yanks went home empty handed and subtly berated.

However, growth in American greyhound racing went on unabated. Following the success of the sport in the USA during the early 1920s, in 1925 Mr Charles Munn came to Britain to once again present the case for greyhound racing, arriving with little more than hope. At first he found scant encouragement, but after meeting Major L. Lyne Dixon, a well-known coursing judge and enthusiast, who was impressed by the possibilities of the sport, Munn began to feel his optimism was vindicated. Dixon worked to convert his coursing friends, and many were less than keen, feeling Munn's vision was alien to the form of the sport pursued with greyhounds in the kingdom from the very earliest times. From the days of Canute and before, greyhounds had been an important feature of British country life. In bygone times these dogs had been regarded as having greater value than many people who occupied the lower echelons of the social strata. But Munn's crusade continued and when he showed pictures of the embryonic American sport to Brigadier General A.C. Critchley, a Canadian living in England, 'Critch' immediately saw its immense possibilities. Racing greyhounds provided an outlet for those who, while loving the dog and admiring its qualities, objected to seeing the death of an animal as the end of it. This was the moral impetus that enabled the financial imperative demonstrated by the growing American evidence of the business potential of greyhound racing. As is nearly always the case, monetary considerations swept aside the doubters and luddites. An organisation called the Greyhound Racing Association (GRA) was established as a limited company in 1926 with Sir William Gentle, a retired chief constable of Brighton, as its first chairman. Critchley put up the £22,000 needed to float the company and build its first racing venue. The first head office was at Belle Vue, Manchester, where the track was to be located. The firm was granted a Stock Exchange quotation for its shares; the initial stock was sold at a shilling (5p) a share.

Whilst Belle Vue was being constructed, greyhounds were recruited from coursing kennels and trained to pursue the dummy hare. On 24 July 1926, Mistley, a dog with half a tail, wearing the blue coat of trap 2, won the first ever greyhound race contested over 440 yards, on a circular track, in Britain. Mistley's margin of victory was eight lengths and he covered the ground in 25 seconds. He was by Jack-in-Office out of a dam named Duck.

That first programme of events, that Winston Churchill was to call 'animated roulette', consisted of three races over 440 yards, two over 500 yards and one over 440-yard hurdles. Melksham Autocrat won this latter contest by ten lengths in 27.8 seconds. Eight dogs contested each race; the British rule (that was not replicated elsewhere) limiting each race to a maximum of six greyhounds was not framed until 1 January 1927. The judge's box was on the inside of the track and the hare was on the outside.

The decision to build the first track in the north was based on the strength of whippet racing in the region, which had been developed by the miners of Lancashire, Yorkshire and Derbyshire. However, this pursuit had been adopted by most working-class communities in the country since the mid-nineteenth century. These small, inexpensive, seemingly fragile, but deceptively tough and brave lightweights, all bones and eyes, were the pets of the poor. Often living in their owner's kitchen and sleeping at the foot of their master's bed, these diminutive racers were set to compete on every patch of wasteland in Britain at one time. It was a relatively well-organised sport, although it lacked the appropriate infrastructure to prevent widespread corruption. But dockers, miners and factory workers made it their own, as did, strangely enough, hangmen. Executioner Jim Billington kept his whippets in the late nineteenth century in Bolton. In the 1920s John Ellis looked after his in Rochdale. In 1923 he was to make the journey down to Holloway Prison to dispatch Edith Thompson, who had, probably wrongly, been convicted of murdering her husband. He couldn't make the scheduled 5 January date for the execution as he had planned to run his whippets on that day, so Thompson's life was extended until 9 January, at the whippet's pleasure.

It was thought that greyhound racing would recruit from the large following of whippets. Yet a crowd of only 1,600 witnessed the first meeting, and of these only about half paid for admission. The GRA lost £50 on that first event, but that would be the exception that proved the rule. The Sporting Chronicle, the leading sporting journal of the time reported:

SUCCESSFUL NEW VENTURE
Greyhound racing, the pursuit of a synthetic hare mechanically propelled around an oval track, was introduced to the sport-loving people of Great Britain with marked promise of prosperity . . . There were capital performances by the dogs . . . People who had not visited the place during public trials* were obviously much impressed by the elaborate setting and ceremonial, and also by the importance attached to the sport throughout. It certainly is a dignified game . . .

* In the week before Belle Vue opened, the greyhounds could be seen acclimatising to the track. This would have been the only chance to assess their abilities.

The apparent indifference of the public to greyhound racing was short lived. Word of the excitement and sport available at the track spread fast, the swiftness of the hounds balanced against the demands of the track, wherein one of a crowd of dogs hit bends at practically the same time at breakneck speed, the search for space in the rush, escaping or getting into difficulties, speeding up and slowing down. This meant that every dog was in with a shout (or a bark), 'all against all and the devil take the hindmost'. It seemed the sublime and perfect gambling sport, and the British workingman loved a bet.

Before the end of the year, Belle Vue was host to crowds of more than 30,000 and those who had faith in the venture were fully justified. The share price now stood at £37 10s – an increase of 750 per cent!

When greyhound racing first began it was confined to the afternoons of the summer months since there was no overhead lighting for winter and evening racing. Three meetings were held each week, the last on 9 October. Celtic Park hosted the first ever venue for greyhound racing meeting in Northern Ireland on 18 April 1927 and the first meeting in London took place at White City on 20 June that year. From this point tracks mushroomed all over Britain and the world. At about the same time as Smith and Munn were initiating greyhound racing in the USA a man with the unfortunate name of Swindell was attempting to launch the sport in New South Wales. The Australian Greyhound Association was granted a licence by the New South Wales Government and the first meeting took place on 28 May 1927, at Harold Park, Sydney. No betting was allowed on what was initially called 'Mechanical Hare Racing'. Only a fortnight after the first Australian meeting the inaugural greyhound racing event in Ireland took place at Shelbourne Park in Dublin.

The Manchester Track
The Greyhound Racing Club

In the English context tracks grew up on the waste grounds of the industrial sprawls of metropolitan areas, some racing seven days a week. During the first complete season of track racing in England, with a full programme at Belle Vue, White City, Harringay and elsewhere, 5,656,686 people paid to go through the turnstiles.

It was around this time that Owen Smith passed away in Miami, having parented 53 dog-track devices and having organised the International Greyhound Racing Association. He died a rich man, the owner of twenty-five tracks in the southern United States. His name is perpetuated in America by the O.P. Smith Classic, which was run at the track of the Miami Beach Club each year.

But track management in Britain had a lot to learn. There were doping scandals, dogs were switched, and razor gangs and protection racketeers harassed the bookmakers. All of which gave ammunition to the anti-gambling elements in British society, headed by the Church. Promoters acted swiftly. The best-run tracks banded together in alliance as the National Greyhound Racing Society (NGRS) from which, in 1928, a governing body emerged, the National Greyhound Racing Club. Rules were drawn up and all members of the NGRS accepted the Club as having complete control over the sport. Stewards administered the new rules, officials were licensed, malpractice was stamped out, and gradually public confidence in the sport was restored.

> In trap 3 there's a hound,
> On whom I've wagered a pound,
> It had a nice name,
> And looks up for the game,
> So I think my investment is sound.
>
> My dog is in white,
> And at first looks all right,
> But on the last fatal bend,
> My story comes to a sad end,
> And all's to be said is 'goodnight!'
>
> From '*The Ballad of the West Ham Dogs*'

2
THE RACING WORLD

Trails

The first directors of the Greyhound Racing Association, Limited, which had its first
headquarters at 19 Tothull Street, Westminster, were Sir W. Gentle, J.P. (chairman), Brigadier-
General A.C. Critchley, C.M.G., D.S.O. (vice-chairman), Mr Robert Grant, Jun., Major L. Lyne
Dixon, Mr F.A. Luni, J.P., and Mr F.S. Gentle.

Croxton Smith, A. (1927) *Greyhound Racing and Breeding*.
Gay and Hancock Ltd, London

Six dogs run round an oval track in pursuit of an artificial, mechanical hare.
The hare is always the first to pass the winning post; what fascinates,
intrigues, mystifies and motivates those who attend the greyhound tracks of
the world is the search for the dog who will most closely follow the synthetic
quarry home.

Six days of the week, every afternoon and every evening of every week
during any peacetime year for nearly eighty years dog racing has been taking
place. People have been watching and betting on every race. On any given day
in contemporary Britain there are a dozen or more greyhound tracks staging
meetings. There are ten or twelve races at each meeting. So, on around 312
days a year there are something like 1,000 dogs running. About £400 million is
gambled each year on the tracks of the United Kingdom. Around £1,600 is
speculated on the six-dog passion in betting shops. Every year in Britain
approximately 50,000 greyhound races are contested. This means that
greyhound racing is near to half-a-million races old in Britain alone and this is
going on right across the world, in Ireland, the USA, Mexico, Australia and
Spain. Greyhound racing is truly an international sport, but more than this it is
a global industry that occupies and fascinates tens of millions of people, for a

moment, a few days in a year, or a lifetime of what some would call devotion, others obsession.

Those tens of thousands of greyhounds whining and scrabbling in their tiny traps in Britain are waiting for what might be thought of as the basic sustenance of the sport. These races, one-lap affairs fought out by run-of-the-mill animals, with a winning prize of not much more than £100, are graded races. The common racing greyhound is a grader. Whilst West Ham was in operation the standard of a graded event was judged by the size of the prize money that it offered. In the late 1970s races were graded by number, usually one to nine. Nine was for puppies and scrubbers and the fliers were designated as a one. It was the racing manager's job to decide what grade of race any particular greyhound would compete in. Most American racetracks subscribe to an automatic grading system that promotes dogs to a superior grade when they win and relegates them to a lower grade when they end up outside the prize money, that is a placing outside the first four, on three consecutive occasions. The grade of the race is indicated in the track programme. Racing forms act as a barometer of each dog's ability.

The racing manager would also assign dogs to traps. There are dogs who prefer to run on the inside, keeping snug to the rails, other animals are wider runners, they look to be clear of other dogs on their inside. There have been no end of theories why one hound likes to be tucked up to the fence and another, out on its own, in the middle of the track, but in the end it is all a matter of personality.

Theoretically, the racing manager's objective is to achieve a dead heat between all runners. In his/her attention to this ambition he/she will draw a railer in trap one or two, whilst the wide runner will be given trap five or six. Traps three and four are the 'hell traps': unless a dog is a really classy performer or just plain lucky coming out of these berths, it can often become squashed as its rivals spring after the hare. As can be guessed, the draw plays an important part in the outcome of any race. If the racing manager consistently draws a greyhound in the 'accursed' middle starting positions, the dog's owner may well become suspicious, feeling that there is a plot afoot. However, if the racing manager draws another animal too often in traps one or six then an equally damning accusation of corruption awaits. Such is the thankless and complex task of those who would manage dog racing. There is, it goes without saying, no solution to the troubles associated with the trap draw. But it is the very spirit of dog-track competition that the body of hounds will be looking to get round a kind of obstacle course of a difficult circuit, with sharp and sudden turns. If this were not the case only the swiftest animal would take the spoils. The fickle ghosts of cunning, intelligence and luck would play little part, thus lessening competitive elements of the sport and in the process the intoxicating spectacle would become a predictable parade.

In the last days of the West Ham greyhound track, races were divided into graded and open events, ranging from 230-yard sprints to 1,200-yard

Controlling the hare
The control tower
Massage will loosen up a canine racer

marathons. Up to six greyhounds may run in a British or Irish race; eight is the usual number in America and Australia. In the early seventies British greyhounds usually raced on grass, but American and Australian tracks always favored a sand surface.

In Britain all but about ten per cent of greyhounds are graders. With racing lives of two or three years, they will likely spend the whole of their brief careers competing in events that will remain in only the most devoted owner's memory. But every now and then, a dog will emerge that is truly whelped under a racing moon. It will shame its comrades and give the racing manager even more headaches, as they will leave the crowd standing every time. This is the animal that will run the gauntlet and skip the veritable light fantastic in open meets. They are the Premiership players of canine competition, the crème de la crème; the feline's gold-top sodden whiskers; the bees most knobbly knees, the proverbial DBs.

On most evenings there are open races running, they are the glamour events and everyone involved in the sport can't get enough of them. A dog has to be approved to be an open racer and the ranks of this elite included the best-graded runners and greyhounds trained in private kennels. These events may be supported by local turf accountants at a small, provincial track with as little as a few dozen rain-soaked punters watching in deluded misery. For their fee a winner may claim a couple of hundred pounds and a silver-plated wine cooler. However, the open race might be the final of a Classic event like the Cesarewitch, taking place at the grandiose and cavernous edifice of West Ham Stadium, where, in front of a cheering crowd of tens of thousands, a weighty trophy and bulging purse will be awarded to the winner.

How much is that doggy . . . ?

There are a number of ways of buying a greyhound. Going to a breeder is a common option but dogs can also be purchased from agents, trainers, at auction or from the back pages of one of the specialist publications. But success cannot be guaranteed, even though knowledge of a good breeder is likely to be the surest way of finding a useful hound. However, such awareness, even with the requisite cash, will not mean that you will come away with the new Bradshaw Fold; in greyhound racing, being in the know is the highest form of insurance. This is really a way of dealing with the problem of chance, a means of rationalizing that which is irrational. If a dog does come from nowhere and starts to take major open races this is put down to the owner or the trainer being in the know. But those who are acknowledged to be in the know are the gurus and aristocracy of the sport wrapped into one. It is the philosophical pinnacle of track life. Many aspire to be in it, others pretend they are in it or have been in it. No one is ever quite sure who is in it, but what is for sure, some are, and their position is enviable but at the same time despised, as the observer of one in the know is acknowledging that they are not.

Handicapping

The search to find a dog capable of running in open races is a challenge, even for the most knowledgeable and educated 'dog person'. To buy a young dog with a chance of being marked on the best race cards would cost near £10,000. An animal that might make a significant impact in such events would be valued much higher.

Unless one is about to train their own greyhound to race, which some do, the first thing any owner must do is find a trainer for their dog. Most trainers are associated with tracks although there are private trainers who work with dogs who will contest open events. Track-based owners will work with some of the graders that compete at the track and maybe some open-race dogs. Each track has a number of trainers associated with it. In the 1950s West Ham had about six or seven but a stadium might contract as many as a dozen trainers. A greyhound will need a minimum of three trials before it can race. A trial might involve one, two or three other animals. When it shows enough speed your greyhound will be placed on a race card. Generally, the better the track the faster the grading time that will be expected of a dog.

A big stadium will give low-grade races a purse of around £80. Top-grade contests will be awarded about £150. At a medium-level track outside the main metropolitan areas the same grades of races will amount to something like £45 and £90. The hound in sixth place will get £20 or £25 for its trouble. These sums would be equivalent to about twenty-five per cent of the equivalent American and Australian winnings, but in both countries there are fewer races, perhaps no more than one meeting each week at any given track. But it would be foolish to race a dog more than once a week; so British owners do not gain on the redoubtable roundabouts of fate what they might lose on destiny's swings of fortune.

Some tracks operate handicap racing, sometimes with eight dogs. Faster runners are penalized by having to start behind slower rivals, traps being staggered. These races have been popular in Scotland and the north of England but have been rarely used elsewhere in Britain. They are more common in Australia where at least eight and sometimes as many as ten animals compete in each race. In theory the handicap system offers each runner a clear path. The

The bends

most efficient racing manager in history could not manage that number of dogs from level traps. Handicapping may be a much fairer system than the charge-and-bustle, fight-for-the-bend histrionics that is racing on most British tracks. However, canine oval racing is a custom as much as it is anything else and as such it adheres to its flaws and imperfections and makes of them a blessing. Imbued in the tradition of the 'if it isn't broke don't fix it' school, and wed to the pragmatics of the 'tried and trusted', entertainment and chance will not give too much ground to the ethics of sporting purity and the morality of noble parity.

Going round the bend

Before a race at West Ham, the runners were fitted with light muzzles and their jackets. After a veterinary examination and identity check in the paddock, the runners were paraded on the track for public inspection and then put in the respective compartments of the starting traps, which had a grilled front. The dummy hare was made out of skins stretched over a frame. It had a bobbing movement and was electrically operated. It passed the traps at speed, tripping a mechanism that automatically opened the front grill to release the greyhounds who had already been alerted by first the noise and then the sight of the lure. During the race, the hare could not be too close to the runners as this caused checking. At the same time the prey had to be prevented from moving too far ahead of the chasing runners, as the dogs could lose sight of it.

Once the race was under way, many factors came into account. Speed was vital, but courage and trackcraft counted for a lot. The ability to negotiate the bends may have been crucial. As dogs could corner at such high speeds enormous pressure was placed on their fragile legs and this was a common cause of injury. Inexperienced runners tended to run wide on corners where clever dogs could gain lengths at these points. The luck of the trap draw also played a part in things; it may have made or marred chances. A wide runner drawn in trap one could badly bump itself and others when swinging out on the critical first bend, where a clash of racing styles could cause major mishaps before the field spread out. Around the second bend and along the back straight a speedy dog had the power to nullify earlier setbacks, though a back-straight specialist may have encountered trouble entering the third bend where front-runners could start to fade. The clever dog, however, had the sense to slip through if openings were presented and on the last bend, where the leaders might have been tiring, railing ability could have gained yards as opponents swung wide.

Once the race was over, the hare was slowed to a halt round the next two bends and covered with a metal lid. An old skin was often thrown to appease the dogs, which were collected by their handlers and returned to the racing kennels or paraded for presentation.

There are a small number of tracks that are extremely tight, with bends wrought at angles so acute that they seem to deny any geometric logic. On these mad circuits no totally wholesome event can be staged. Their shape and size are of massive variation, made, it seems, to be unique more than for any other purpose, but as a group they can offer a one-lap race of about 470m. A greyhound will cover this distance in approximately half a minute. This 'four-bend' affair is what most greyhounds are attuned to, and are signified by an 'A' in a race programme, A1, A2 and so on. Less common are the 'S' events. These are six-bend, 650m journeys, contested over one-and-three-quarter laps in around forty seconds. The educated owner will have preference for a dog that will run half-a-dozen bends well, not only because they give a longer run for their keep, but also the elongated race can cancel out any advantages or disadvantages of trap draw or poor starts. In these races greyhounds can recover from being boxed, bulked and checked and go on to take the race.

Hurdle races are a variation within the above themes. They are popular, especially in Britain. The jumps present a thrilling display, and greyhounds that lose interest on the flat often take on a new lease of life over the barriers.

Racing greyhounds wear jackets. The colours of this attire, as with the silks worn by racing jockeys, aid the separation of dog from dog. Trap one is fire red, two is cold blue, the three remains pure in white, four is donned in ominous black, five flies from the trap in mystic orange, whilst the notorious six-dog is humbugged in black and white stripes. There are any number of tales about how these hues were established. There are 'dog-people' who will tell you the uniforms were designated by Satan in a deal that included the soul of one of the Lord Orford's, in exchange for a Waterloo Cup winner. 'Ben the Bishop', who, on race nights, sold the *Greyhound Express* outside the West Ham dog track, would recite the story that would tell how King Solomon had sorted the dog's wardrobes out. The six-dog's suit mirrored the royal colours of Tutankhamun, he being the first to dress his dogs in the colours of the Magpie, which like the greyhound was sacred in the beliefs of the 'Boy King'. However, what is for sure, the number and its accompanying colours are, for the duration of any race, synonymous with name, form, characteristics and history of a racing dog. As such, the vagueness of choice is clarified or compounded

The racing kennels

according to your own human skill, mood or inclination, but in the end they let the observer know as quickly as possible the outcome of the race.

This is especially necessary in sprint events, when 250m are covered in fifteen seconds. The hounds that smash out these races are the rockets of the breed. Middle-distance or 550m are done and dusted in around thirty-five seconds whilst marathons of sometimes a bit more than 800m last in the region of fifty-three seconds. All these times are approximations of course. A rough animal and a top dog can be separated by two to four seconds, but even a sluggish greyhound will leave the fittest human behind from the start. The lowly creature ranked A9 will still clock something near forty miles an hour, as fast as the speedway bikes of the 1940s and 1950s that shared the facilities of West Ham Stadium with greyhounds.

International dogs

Although many champions have been bred in Britain – Derby winners Trev's Perfection, Narrogar Ann, and Ford Spartan, to name a few – Ireland is where, historically, most English owners have looked for potential stars. Because breeders have always carefully retained their best bitches for breeding and so many Irish stud dogs, such as Tanist, have dominated breeding lines, Ireland has produced some of the best blood lines. In addition, the Emerald Isle is generally thought to be more suitable for rearing greyhounds that thrive on being allowed to roam free all day in open country.

Because of its history of strict quarantine laws, international racing in Britain has been difficult. However, Anglo-Irish international races have taken place in both countries (there are around twenty tracks in Ireland) and teams from Britain and Ireland are sent to race permanently in America and also in Spain.

William F. Cody, the famous 'Buffalo Bill', can be credited as having a major part to play in the introduction of greyhounds into America, being influential in the founding of the American stock on which greyhound racing was developed in the USA. Cody's friend General James Custer, famous for his last stand against Sitting Bull, and who Cody was to later employ as a member of the cast of his Wild West show, was also a breeder of greyhounds. Before Cody brought the Wild West show to Britain in 1889, Custer asked his friend to bring him back two well-bred greyhounds, a dog and bitch. The general's aim was to breed from this gift. Cody went to Colonel North's famous kennels to purchase the dog Dingwall, which had that year run up for the Waterloo Plate, and the bitch Miss Kitten. Whether or not Cody kept them or had half the resulting litter is not known, but several of the pups, among which was Border Ruffian, appeared in the American Greyhound Stud Book in the name of W.F. Cody.

Although the United States can be understood to be the birthplace of the sport, of the 160-odd tracks constructed between 1920 and 1930 less than fifty are still in operation. At its height there were more than twenty-five racing venues in Florida, the most important track being the West Flagler circuit at Miami, a quarter-mile track with an inside hare. Equally important was the Miami Beach Kennel Club Stadium. At these two tracks annual attendance often passed the million mark, with tote takings of more than $50 million. Similar figures may be quoted for the Southland Park Stadium at West Memphis, Arkansas, for the Wonderland Park Stadium, Revere, Boston, and for the Taunton track; the last two tracks were both opened in 1935.

Most American states that legalized totalisator betting limited it to days only, thus prohibiting wagering at night when the greyhounds, which had difficulty competing with horse-racing during the day, might run. However, although the greyhound racing was legal in only seven states, in the last quarter of the twentieth century it was the seventh largest spectator sport in America. In Florida, where it was the state's largest spectator sport, it attracted more than four million people a year to 18 tracks. The most important races in the United States were the US $125,000 Flagler International and the American Derby over 660 yards. Both were open to greyhounds from any tracks in America or other countries.

The American-bred greyhound is a great sprinter, but it cannot match the Irish-bred dogs for stamina. Most of the country's breeders are found in the states of Kansas, Texas, Oklahoma, Nebraska, Missouri and Arkansas, and some greyhounds come from Canada and Australia. In the USA, jacket colours are different and the eight-dog format creates a number of variations in the betting culture, including the 'show' bet which pay out on a third plane.

Greyhounds have been part of Australia since its discovery by Captain Cook in 1770. He carried greyhounds on the *Endeavour*. Live hare coursing as a sport first started in the New South Wales country town of Orange in 1897, a bitch with the unlikely name of Bunny won the first event. Live hare coursing is now banned in every state, but all states run mechanical-hare greyhound racing. The first of these meetings was held at the Harold Park track in Sydney on a May night in 1927. A week on, the first daylight meeting was held. Twelve days later for the first time bookmakers took part in a greyhound meeting. Church opposition, however, helped persuade the government to ban night meetings after only six months, and eventually the ban was extended to all meetings. It was 1931 before the prohibition was revoked, but night meetings were still illegal in Queensland as greyhound racing disappeared from London's East End in 1971.

From the introduction of Australia's off-course tote greyhound racing enjoyed unprecedented popularity. In the final decades of the twentieth century in New South Wales alone there were an average of five meetings a day with prize money for the year well in excess of $A1.25 million. The richest race was the National Greyhound Sprint Championship, which had its first running in 1969. It carried $A21,000 prize money. Following elimination races the fastest dogs from each state were selected to run in the finals in Sydney. There were not quite 100 tracks in Australia (about half were in New South Wales), and these supported important races like the Wentworth Park (Sydney) Derby and the Australian Greyhound Cup.

Australia has produced some of the world's fastest greyhounds. Their times, usually set on hard-packed damp sand tracks, have astounded foreign visitors. The finest effort by one of these champions was at Harold Park in 1944, when Chief Havoc attempted to set six different track records from 440 yards to 880 yards. Over 17,000 people saw him break five and equal the sixth. Another leading greyhound was Zoom Top, Australia's number one prizewinner with almost $A60,000 when she retired in 1970. A consistent performer, she won races in four different states from 310 yards to 870 yards against the best greyhounds from every part of Australia. She ran record times on 16 occasions.

Doping and ringing

Since the start of the greyhound racing, a constant battle has been fought against dopers, and trainers are constantly on the alert against the doping menace. In the modern sport doping attempts are rare, and even if the security barrier is ever breached, chromatography is the ultimate safeguard. This mini-laboratory is installed at many courses and is used for tests of the greyhounds when they arrive at the track. Traces of dope can be detected minutes after tests on urine samples. Should a test be positive, the greyhound is withdrawn from the meeting and a full inquiry by stewards and security officers is held.

Greyhounds can also be made to run slower by being fed a heavy meal before racing, though this method would soon be detected as every dog is officially weighed before the start of a race. Too great a variation from its last weight means a dog will be withdrawn. Other frauds have involved 'ringing', the slang term for switching a runner with a faster, almost identical dog. Not uncommon in the sport's early days, the practice was effectively stamped out by the introduction of greyhound identity books, which contain details of ownership, breeding, and the complete markings and colours of the dog right down to its toenails.

However, one Australian greyhound did not even give officials the opportunity to test it. Part-owners both doped the dog without telling the other. One used caffeine and the other amphetamine – a combination that did not have the desired effect. The dog collapsed and died before it reached the start.

Mourn for the black dog in the cursed trap 4,
Weep as his foe close the race door,
Crushed and crowded, greyhound sandwich is he,
Locked in the middle, longing to be free.

But his dark eyes will search for the light,
This shadow, this omen, will struggle and fight,
And every now and then, this squashed dark sinner,
Will leap to the front and come home a winner.

From *'The Ballad of the West Ham Dogs'*

3
COCKNEY DOGS

'Entry Badge'

To get the men and raise the capital was but the beginning. Of equal importance was the question of finding the dogs to compete. It was not so easy as it sounds, the number of greyhounds being somewhat limited. In the twenty-two years ending 1914, 89,636 were registered in the Greyhound Stud Book, the aggregate for 1914 being 5,553.

Croxton Smith, A. (1927) *Greyhound Racing and Breeding*.

Gay and Hancock Ltd., London

The area of East London where West Ham Stadium, the site of West Ham Greyhound Track, had a 'canine-based' tradition of gaming and sporting activity long before the arena was built. The land the track would occupy was, at the turn of the twentieth century, Custom House football ground. The facility included a cinder track that was used for whippet racing. Owners prepared their dogs for a race by teasing them into a frenzy by waving a sack in their faces. Each dog was held by the collar and tail and 'slipped' on the firing of the starting gun. They would then dash down the track beyond a winning line. These events, which attracted huge crowds, were served by a range of clandestine bookies who, for the most part, benefited from the local representatives of the law turning a blind eye.

Sprint races were held on the primitive West Ham track on most Sunday mornings. These were organised into handicap sixty-yard dashes against the clock. Usually there were eight, four-runner heats that provided semi-finals and a final. These events were also the focus of the gambling fraternity. Regular training took place at the track with recognised 'instructors', many of whom were part of gambling cartels involved in 'arranging form'.

The Lodger meets The Winker

The East Enders did not confine themselves to 'single species' events. On one occasion a race between a whippet and a racing pigeon took place. The dog's owner and trainer was Mr Reginald Revins, a 'snow clearer' by trade. His pride and joy was The Lodger, a whippet that had known a deal of success on the racing circuit and was something of a champion. The pigeon, Gonkin's Tangerine, affectionately known as 'The Winker', came from the loft of Harry H. Harold, a foreman from the local slaughterhouse. Despite the fact that it only had one eye, the bird had distinguished itself on many occasions. The Winker's success, it was rumoured, was, at least in part, due to a 'racing diet' that included scraps of fish batter and chips. The Tangerine was known for his bravery and tenacity. He had reputedly injured himself during a long distance race and walked the last mile-and-a-half to his home nest and as such completed the contest.

The dog *v.* bird event was contested over 100 yards; both animals were slipped by hand from the starting line. Many people thought that Gonkin would soar skyward without delay, leaving The Lodger to dash to the finishing line. The bookies were dealing with long queues waiting to place bets, most of which were on the whippet. When the gun went, The Lodger was off in a flash whilst Tangerine swerved violently across the track and then, accompanied by a huge cheer, made for the clouds. At the halfway stage, The Lodger was yards ahead, whilst The Winker fluttered high above the track. But as the whippet closed in on the finish, the penny seemed to drop and the pigeon plummeted with it. Gonkin's Tangerine swooped alongside The Lodger and broke into full flight, holding a height about four feet above the ground. With a few powerful flaps of its wings, the feathered avenger simply shot past the dogged dog to win by a distance.

The shame was to be too much for Revins. It was said that he parted with his dog in exchange for a pony and trap and left the area. Harold, to be known from then on as Harry the Trackster, won a considerable amount of money on the race and later set up a fish and chip shop in Canning Town; his 'The Winker's Fish Supper' remained a local favourite for years to come. Harold was to keep his association with dog-racing, investing in many a good running whippet and had family connections with the Donachy Bookmaking Empire based in East Ham. Gonkin's Tangerine died, as he would have wanted, in competition, but his demise was tinged with ironic tragedy. The Winker was run over by a pony and trap whilst taking a breather near Wrotham in Kent, towards the finish of a marathon event that had started in Rome. As such he will always remain a champion of 'The Eternal City'. The Lodger continued to race for a number of years under the ownership of a gypsy family who resided on Bonny Downs, Barking. However towards the end of his competitive career he was bought by Charlie Relf, owner of the Old Imperial (formally The Royal Albert music hall) in Canning Town. The Lodger became something of a favourite at this venue, more widely known as Relf's, after the owner. Relf's was advertised in *The Stage* as the handsomest and most comfortable [music hall] in East London, entirely lit by electricity. The hall had its own built-in pub, The Town of Ayr, and engaged acts at enormous expense. These included Tom Costelleo, famous for the ditty 'At Trinity Church I Met me Doom'; Charlie Coborn who wowed audiences with his 'Two Lovely Black Eyes' and 'The Man that Broke the Bank at Monte Carlo'. Kate Carney, the voice behind 'Three Pots a Shilling', also trod the boards at Relf's as did Vesta Victoria whose rendition of 'Waiting at the Church' was a national hit. Other favourites at the Old Imperial were Gus Elen who had great success with 'It's a Great Big Shame', and Ella Shields, the original 'Burlington Bertie from Bow'.

The Lodger appeared in the pantomime Dick Whittington at the Imperial; in that particular version Dick's usual sycophantic and demonstrative cat was replaced by a belligerently miserable, inanimate whippet, no doubt in mourning for his more distinguished track days. However, his demeanour caught the eye of the Scottish silent movie director, celebrant and pioneer of the Scottish/Yiddish cinemagraphic social realist movement, Pandy McGinsburg. He saw the Lodger as perfect for his short feature *The Wee Scabby Dawg*, a cinematic parable about a waif abandoned to the cruelties of Glasgow street life. For a while it looked as if The Lodger would become a household name north of the border, but it was not to be. Whilst in transit from London to the McGinsburg's studio in Ayrshire, his drivers decided to take a break from their journey and stopped at a café in Halifax. The Lodger was tied to a railing outside to 'stretch his legs'. However, when the van got to its destination it was realised that the wonder whippet had been left lashed to its northerly station. Efforts were made to retrieve the poor misplaced mongrel, but to no avail. As such, a starlet was thwarted and the world was never to see the making of the canine equivalent of Buster Keaton.

West Ham Stadium

The West Ham track opened for operation in 1928. It was one of the first of the London tracks, and with Stamford Bridge one of the fastest in Britain. At one time the track at West Ham boasted eight world records over various distances. It was the longest circuit in the country with a circumference of 562 yards. It had long straights and wide, sweeping, well-banked bends, as such fighting amongst the greyhounds, a perennial threat in those days, was almost unknown. The dogs taking part in races over the standard 550 yards did not even complete a full circuit of the West Ham oval. The track was unique too in that the entire running surface was raised on wood 12 inches above the ground. It had a matting surface imported from Sweden and just needed watering to keep it in good condition. However, some owners and trainers refused to run on it, as it would break three or four hocks a year. This is somewhat ironic given the modern toll on hocks, some tracks claiming 50 hocks a year. This 'track architecture' gave West Ham three major

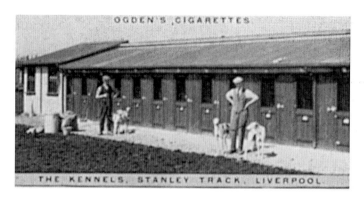

The kennels

advantages:
– Racing was fast, even in the most sodden of winter conditions
– 'Time' variations were extremely small and this made forecasting a more
  straightforward process
– Meetings could take place in most conditions – at West Ham, event
  cancellations were relatively rare.

West Ham stadium could accommodate a crowd of 100,000, all of whom would have a clear view of the whole racing circuit. An excellent restaurant and refreshment bars in each enclosure catered for spectators.

Greyhound racing was first held at West Ham Stadium at 8p.m. on 4 August 1928. The opening event was advertised in the *East Ham Echo* the day before as taking place in, 'The latest, largest and most comfortable Greyhound Stadium Course in England'. It told the readers that special West Ham Tram Corp. Services for the stadium would be running on race nights and that accommodation for over 100,000 spectators (mostly under cover) was available. It went on to boast of the permanent luxurious kennels for over 100 dogs. Admission fees were given as 1/2 (under 6p), 2/4 (about 12p) and 5 shillings (25p); this included insurance. A special bank holiday meeting was also advertised for the Monday along with directions of how to get there:

Rail (L.N.E.R) to Custom House and 5 mins walk: Underground to Plaistow and change to trams: Buses to Green Gate, Barking Rd. (7 mins walk: Trams – L.C.C. to Green Gate, West Ham Trams to Stadium.

Subsequent advertisements included the motto, 'Within easy reach of all parts' and the assurance that events were conducted under N.G.R.C. rules. During the summer months the West Ham promotion was placed above a plea to 'Buy Coal Now at Lowest Summer Prices'.

When the hare first ran

The report of the first meeting at West Ham was given in the 10 August 1928 edition of the *East Ham Echo* under the strap line, 'Greyhound Racing – Opening of the New Course at West Ham Stadium'. The new greyhound racecourse track at West Ham Stadium was opened on Saturday evening, with a programme of seven races. There was an attendance of 56,000 – a record crowd for the sport.

Despite the threatening clouds and the rain earlier in the afternoon, the weather in the evening was fine, and the course was in excellent condition. The roads leading to West Ham Stadium were crowded and a constant stream of spectators flowed through the turnstiles. The terraces, stands and enclosures were crowded, and the first race on the programme was eagerly looked forward to. The bookmakers in the enclosures found no scarcity of people ready to back their fancies.

Sir Louis William Dane, chairman of the directors, declared the track open with a brief speech which was broadcast to all portions of the ground, and expressed the hope that it would provide them with some excellent sport.

The hare was given a trial run around the course, and the entry of the dogs for the first race – the Romford Stakes – was announced by a cheering fanfare on the trumpet. The dogs entered were Major Shrove, Mooney, Belle O'Brandon, Join Labour, and Ardnaculla Boy. They were released from the starting box as the hare flashed past, and started off in hot pursuit. About a quarter of the distance had been covered when Major Shrove and Ardnaculla Boy started fighting. The other dogs slowed and stopped but again set off in pursuit of the hare. The event was declared 'no race', and was run again after the last race, and Major Shrove and Ardnaculla Boy were disqualified. The second attempt to run the race proved successful, and Mooney came in first with Belle O'Brandon second.

Miss Ryan's 'Glorious Eve' started a hot favourite for the Ilford Stakes, and won the race with ease, with C.S. Casale's Jack Swift second.

The Custom House Stakes, one of the two hurdle races on the programme, proved a popular event, and Mr De Groot's Dribbleit was a good favourite. The race started well, and the favourite secured a good lead from the first hurdle. At the second hurdle King David fell and Killymoon Sport challenged the leader. They took the last two hurdles together and in the straight Killymoon Sport got in front to win from Dribbleit by a head.

The Stratford Stakes

Beacontree Fly and Beacontree Queen were scratched from the Stratford Stakes, and A.H. Briggs' Last Choice started favourite. He was challenged early by Sunny Trace, who looked like winning until being baulked in the finishing straight when trying to cut between Last Choice and Kyrie Sweep. Last Choice came in first with Kyrie Sweep second, and Sunny Trace third.

The Barking Stakes

Hurry Belle made the best time of the evening in the Barking Stakes, which she won from Jecorin in 33.16 seconds. She started a good favourite, and had the race well in hand right from the start.

The A.G.R. Hurdles followed, and produced a good race. The dogs kept well together for three-quarters of the distance, and then Rambler's Hope and Coote Hill forged ahead. Rambler's Hope got in front at the last hurdle, and won by a length.

The Plaistow Stakes

The Plaistow Stakes was the last race on the programme, and Jimmie's Pet started favourite. None of the other dogs were much fancied, and the betting on them ranged from 3-1 to 6-1. Cheerful Chang, an outsider, overhauled the favourite at the half distance and they came into the finishing straight together. Here Cheerful Chang was bumped, and dropped back into third place, Jimmie's Pet winning from Marlfield.

The meeting was splendidly organised, and the whole programme was carried through without the slightest hitch. It was quite apparent that the sport would become extremely popular in the district, and that the West Ham Stadium would probably attract the largest dog-racing crowds in London.   The officials were: Director of Racing, Capt. W.J. Neilson; stewards, Mr J. Collyer Bristow, Capt. R.H.W. Davidson, Col. J.W. Leake, C.M.G., and Commander C.R. Dane; Judge, Mr A.J. Leslie Thompson; racing manager, Mr P.D. Poole; starter, Mr A. Smith; time-keeper, Capt. Ernest Holland, M.C.; Resident Vet. Surgeon Lt-Col. F. Fail.

The birth of a Classic

It was not long before West Ham Stadium had a regular weekly schedule of events. In 1928 speedway took place on Thursday evenings and Saturday afternoons, allowing greyhound meetings to take place on Monday, Wednesday and Saturday evenings, and soon 'the dogs' took their place within East End life. *The East Ham Echo* initiated a column devoted to the sport. The edition of 19 October 1928 was taken up with at the early stages of the first big event to be organised at the track – the inaugural Cesarewitch:

DOGS TO FOLLOW AT WEST HAM STADIUM
Great Interest taken in Greyhound Cesarewitch

Saturday's Meeting

The Greyhound Cesarewitch had been the means of attracting great crowds to the West Ham Stadium during the past week, and visitors have had the opportunity of seeing some of the finest dogs from all tracks in the country.

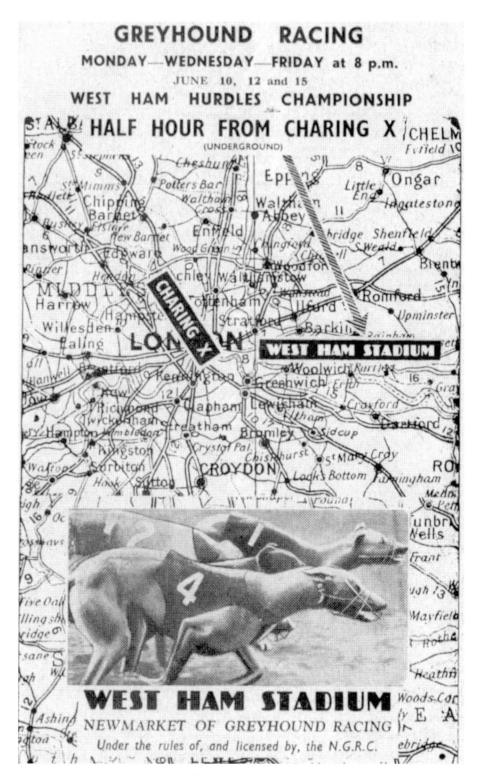

GREYHOUND RACING

MONDAY—WEDNESDAY—FRIDAY at 8 p.m.

JUNE 10, 12 and 15

WEST HAM HURDLES CHAMPIONSHIP

HALF HOUR FROM CHARING X

(UNDERGROUND)

WEST HAM STADIUM

NEWMARKET OF GREYHOUND RACING

Under the rules of, and licensed by, the N.G.R.C.

How to get there.

The semi-finals, which included in one race, such dogs as Autumn Shower, Dick's Son, Hertford, and Brilliant Gambler, give some idea of the popularity of the event with owners.

Dick's Son, which was one of the dogs I mentioned last week, created a world record for speed on the West Ham track during the week.

At the time of writing it is impossible to say which dogs will appear in the final on Saturday night but if the final includes NONSUCH, Autumn Shower, Dick's Son, Hertford, Brilliant Gambler and Corberry's Chieftain, my particular fancy would be NONSUCH.

I should place the West Ham Dog, Brilliant Gambler, which has come with a brilliant record from the North, as second.

The final on Saturday night will undoubtedly draw crowds from all parts of London. It is an event unparalleled in greyhound racing history.

Other dogs which I recommend to be closely watched are: KIRTON DOLL; BLUE CHARLEY; CLUTCHING HAND; FUN FAIR; TEARAWAY; EXPEDITE

The Cesarewitch was always the last Classic of the year; run in October, it boasted the finest and largest trophy ever designed for a greyhound race. Made of pure silver it was West Ham's own creation. It stood 3ft in height and weighed over 300oz. Today it must be one of the most valuable trophies presented on any sporting occasion. The race was also to carry a prize, £1,000 after the war and more than £1,500 in the last days of the Classic at West Ham.

Until the Second World War, apart from 1936, when it was run over 550 yards, the Cesarewitch was run over 600 yards. Post-war, until 1950, the event again asked for 550 yards of commitment. From 1951 until West Ham closed, the trophy was decided over 600 yards. Only the St Leger was then run over a longer distance.

It seems that the Classic was a success from the start. In the East Ham Echo (23 October 1928) under the headline, 'Dogs to Follow at West Ham', our correspondent, now naming himself as 'Trackster', no doubt 'developing his profile', reported:

> The Cesarewitch final at West Ham stadium last Saturday night attracted a great crowd, in spite of the weather's vagaries. It was a night full of good racing, and there is little doubt that this big event has increased the popularity of the West Ham Stadium with owners and public alike.

Whilst Trackster seemed to have edged his bets fairly thoroughly, Dick's Son did win the first Classic event at West Ham in a respectable time of 34.38 seconds.

Blooming dogs

Success of course breeds success as Trackster demonstrated in the same column:

New dogs are constantly being sent to the kennels, and some of the finest dogs in the country are gradually being established here.

The Echo had illustrated this effect in a previous edition (19 October 1928):

A new arrival at West Ham Stadium is Mr Heigh Donachy's Magic Band, which is in Green's kennels.

It seems ownership was something of a family affair:

'CLUTCHING HAND'
Mr S. Donachy of East Ham, the owner of 'Clutching Hand', which is in Green's kennels at West Ham Stadium, has entered this dog for the Irish Produce Stakes.
   'Clutching Hand', which has shown excellent form on the track, is a fine coursing dog. (ibid)

This movement to West Ham is a testament to the fine kennels included in the stadium complex, but the final sentence shows that although the coming of a Classic event to West Ham may have signalled the establishment of the new era of greyhound sport, there had not been a sudden break with the past. There was a crossover or transition period wherein dogs were taking part in racing and coursing events.

The *East Ham Echo* also confirmed that the ownership of West Ham dogs was up for grabs:

GREYHOUNDS FOR AUCTION
Great interest is being centred in the first of the fortnightly sales arranged at West Ham Stadium, to be held on Friday. Each dog will have a trial on the track with the mechanical hare before being put up for auction.
   The trials will start at 10.30, and the sales will commence at eleven. Some of the finest dogs in the country are included among the 100 entries received.

This may well have been a coincidence, but making greyhounds available to local people or people with local interests would have had the effect of creating an affinity with the area. Indeed, a number of individuals from the surrounding locality did make investments. The sale was a great success according to Trackster in the *Echo* (23 October 1928):

At the inaugural auction sale held at the Stadium last Friday good prices were fetched for many of the hundred dogs put up for sale. Towards the end of the sale buyers became very keen, and Mr Hugh Donachy, the well-known East Ham bookmaker, bought Resplendent from Mrs Clements for

110 guineas. Resplendent is a lovely dog, and Mr Donachy will assuredly get his purchase price from stakes the dog is likely to win. I would advise all readers to take a note of him, and await his running.

Mr H. Watts bought Proud Mons for 100 guineas. This is another sound and honest dog whose running should be watched. Mr Watts also bought Chalfont Boy, a favourite at West Ham, the purchase price being 85 guineas. Mrs Prince secured Fees for 75 guineas, and Mr Geoffrey Gilbey sold Gossipping Geoff (late Eight of Clubs) to Mr J. Nathan, a local owner for 55 guineas.

The next sale will take place on Friday week.

Return of the whippets

Trackster, under the heading of 'Whippets To-Night – Experimental Meeting on Greyhound Track – Six Selections for Next Week's Racing' (ibid) testified to yet another early innovation at West Ham:

To-night (Friday) the whippets are to have a chance under the same rules as their bigger brothers, the greyhounds. This is an innovation, and the West Ham Stadium directors are allowing the newly-formed London and South of England Centre of the English Professional Association to run a meeting of eight events, with hurdle races on Friday. The latter body will be responsible for the event and the meeting is being watched with the greatest interest. Doubtless a big crowd will be present.

The whippets have done very well in trials with the electric hare, and it remains to be seen how they perform under artificial light.

I would recommend the following six dogs to be closely watched during the coming week: RESPLENDENT; CLUTCHING HAND; BRILLIANT GAMBLER; KEASH EAGLE; BLUE CHARLIE; CHASE ME CHARLIE.

West Ham was probably not the best place to run whippets. The little dogs seemed lost in the great stadium, but it created novelty interest, something the arena was never afraid to initiate.

Dog mess

However, 1928 was not wholly a glorious year for greyhound racing. In fact, it was at this time that the sport suffered its first major crisis. Racing had, at first, operated with a monopoly for bookmakers, but the mechanical totalisator was introduced with the Racecourse Betting Act of 1928. This Act legalised gambling for the first time, making the new 'tote' legal on horseracing tracks, but it did not mention greyhound racing. Despite this, totes were installed at tracks all over the country, breaking the stranglehold on track betting that the bookmakers had held onto so tightly. Antagonised by this, the bookies brought

RACING
THROUGHOUT JUNE

every

MONDAY,

WEDNESDAY,

FRIDAY at 8 p.m.

RACING THIS MONTH
EVERY
MONDAY and WEDNESDAY

**London's Largest Track with
every convenience and comfort.**

ADMISSION : 1/3; 2/-; 2/6; 5/-

(Licenced by, and racing under the rules of, the National Greyhound
Racing Club).

GREYHOUND RACING

THROUGHOUT JULY

every

MONDAY and

WEDNESDAY

8 Races.   8 p.m.

See Greyhound Racing
at its best on
ENGLAND'S LARGEST TRACK

— MONDAY NEXT —
ANERLEY STAKES . . . 525 yds. flat

WEST HAM STADIUM
NEWMARKET OF GREYHOUND RACING
Under the rules of, and licensed by, the N.G.R.C.

All next month
RACING EVERY

**MONDAY, WEDNESDAY,
FRIDAY**

First race 8 p.m.   **Eight races**

MONDAY
SELDOM LED STAKES
525 yards FLAT

ADMISSION : 1/3; 2/-; 2/6; 5/-

(Licenced by, and racing under the rules of, the National Greyhound
Racing Club).

a case against one track, and eventually won it on appeal. Another case was won in Scotland. The greyhound tote seemed doomed and the future of the sport looked grim. Public sympathy for a greyhound tote made the government promise new legislation, although as it turned out, everyone had to wait for half a decade for anything to happen.

The Classic continues

The Stratford Express (12 October 1929) marked the coming of the second Cesarewitch with a summary of the early heats:

GREYHOUND CESAREWITCH

The preliminary heats in connection with the Greyhound Cesarewitch Gold Cup over 600 yards at West Ham Stadium were commenced on Monday. The large entry received for this event must be very encouraging to the stadium officials, for it has attracted many of the best greyhounds in the country. Monday's winners and seconds were: Heat 1: 1, Loughnagare (trap 4); 2, Musical Box (trap 2); neck, 35.23 sec. Heat 2: 1, Century Mark (trap 2); 2, Lido Blue (trap 4); 4 lengths, 35.63 sec. Heat 3: 1, Nobleman (trap 1); 2, Conductor (trap 4): 12 lengths, 35.09 sec. Heat 4: 1, Baalbec Arch (trap 3) and Brief Enchantment (trap 4); dead-heat, 35.34 sec. Heat 5: 1, Latest Speed (trap 5); 2, Labour Leader (trap 1); neck, 35.72 sec.

On Wednesday evening the results were mainly in accordance with expectations, the only upset being in the eighth heat, in which Gay Cavalier, a well-known performer at West Ham, but now trained privately, beat the White City dog, Melkaham Endurance. Heat 6: 1, Flying Gift (trap 2); 2, Bombay (trap 3); head, 35.48 sec. Heat 7: 1, Bradshaw Fold (trap 2); 2, Minemoa (trap 1); 7 lengths, 35.16 sec. Heat 8: 1, Gay Cavalier (trap 4); Melkaham Endurance (trap 1); 1 1/2 lengths, 35.61 sec. Heat 9: 1, Starman (trap 1); 2, Apollo the Romeo (trap 4); 10 lengths, 35.87 sec. Heat 10: Trump (trap 3); 2, Borrowed Chimes (trap 4); 2 1/2 lengths, 35.61 sec.

The eventual winner of the trophy was Five of Hearts whose sire was the great Jamie. This dog was the first important sire of racing greyhounds that was also the sire of Mutton Cutlet, who was second to none in terms of providing quality and quantity of champions when mated to a range of bitches. A black brindled son of Jamie out of Miss Cinderella, Mutton Cutlet was whelped in March 1921 and was bred by Major McCalmont. The dog competed in the Waterloo Cup in 1923, 1924 and 1925 and ran well even though he was never able to reach the final. However, he achieved the runner-up position for the Waterloo Plate in 1924. Not long after this he was bought by Tom Morris, keeper of the Irish Stud Book, and put to stud at a fee of 10 guineas. He was mated to very few bitches during his first two or three years of stud life, but by the time of his death in November 1934 he had sired no less than 522 track and course

The White City track

winners. Mutton Cutlet's progeny were involved in 1,218 stake finals. His sons also became exceptional sires: Valiant Cutlet, Mr Moon, Beef Cutlet and his offspring, and many others.

Mr Morris always said that his dog was highly-strung and shy of strangers but loved those he knew well. He will be recalled as one of the best sires of track champions of the early years of the sport.

Jamie was also the sire of Entry Badge, winner of the first English Greyhound Derby, the first Classic event. It was only right that the premier event in the greyhound calendar, and the first event to be given Classic status, was allocated to the White City, headquarters of the GRA and the first track to open in London. The first Derby was run over 500 yards; thereafter until 1975 it was run over 525 yards.

Entry Badge was a good looking brindle, tipping the scales at 69 pounds when he won the first ever Greyhound Derby. His dam was Beaded Nora, a daughter of the great coursing dog Hopsack. Edwin Baxter, the first of the coursing men to believe that track racing had a future, had given 40 guineas for the pup. From his breeding alone much was to be expected of this dog.

Entry Badge was one of three dogs and a bitch born to Beaded Nora in January 1926. As noted above, this was the year track racing began in Britain. Kennelled at the White City, in June 1927 Entry Badge was at that stadium on its opening evening. He won the first trophy, the White City Cup, which was presented to his owner after the dog had defeated the more experienced animals from Belle Vue in a convincing manner. He destroyed the opposition, taking victory by eight lengths in 30.13 seconds over the 525 yards course, and was to remain unbeaten during his first full year of racing.

That first Derby was held on 15 October 1927. However, since then it has been held in late June. Entry Badge won his heat and final by six and a half lengths, one of the largest margins up to that time. Baxter's dogs finished first, second and third; Ever Bright and Elder Brother followed Entry Badge home, though Joe Harmon trained only Entry Badge. He was drawn in trap 5 for the final and started at 1-4, the hottest favourite ever for the event. The next dog to win from the 5 trap was Daw's Dancer in 1953.

For his success in the Derby, Entry Badge won £1,000 for his owner, a very considerable sum in those days. This was the first four-figure prize awarded for a greyhound race.

Entry Badge raced for the best part of two years and was beaten only once. In all he won eleven out of twelve races in the top class. He was one of the fastest ever dogs out of the traps, but he also had the same type of intelligence exhibited by Mick the Miller. He was able to take advantage of any opportunity to move to the rails and he was always able to steer clear of trouble at the turns. He was odds-on favourite in every race he ran. It was usual for him to win by three lengths or more and achieve times that would be considered acceptable even today. Within four months of winning the Derby, he earned £1,500 in prize money. Entry Badge had become the first great champion track-racing greyhound and was the earliest star of the track in the first years of the sport.

So, Five of Hearts, the second winner of West Ham's Cesarewitch, came from a blue-blooded line that would link many champions of the future.

ENTRY BADGE		June 1924 brindled dog
Jamie	Beaded Brow	Earl's Court Asphyxy
	Jibstay	Long Span Chignon
Beaded Nora	Hopsack	Heart of Freedom Beaded Brow
	Beaded Lil	Badoura

Orange is the mystic dog in trap 5,
An inside runner, on the rail he will thrive.
A Buddhist, a Guru, a hound of Zen,
Will bide his time, meditate and then,
On a mantra of speed a lesson he will teach,
And move to victory's Nirvana, far out of reach.

From '*The Ballad of the West Ham Dogs*'

4
THE MILLER'S TAIL

'Mick the Miller'

In the years following the Great War the figures, understandably, fell, partly owing to the fact that coursing men in the Irish Free State broke away from the parent body. In the 1926 volume the Greyhound Stud Book, 2,712 dogs were registered, and 576 litters. However, starting in 1927 the numbers recovered mainly due to the effect of greyhound racing, since only dogs registered or eligible for registration in the Stud Book were allowed to compete. What constitutes eligibility was set out in the Code of Rules of the National Coursing Club (Mr H.A. Groom, 11, Haymarket, SW1).

Croxton Smith, A. (1927) *Greyhound Racing and Breeding.*
Gay and Hancock Ltd., London

The Miller's tail was the best view most greyhounds got of the legendary Mick, the winner of the 1930 Cesarewitch. Mick the Miller won the event in a time of 34.11 but he established a world record in his heat of 34.01 seconds.

With such performances it was becoming clear that track-based events were taking over from coursing in terms of public interest and that speed was beginning to take precedence over hunting cunning in the development and breeding of greyhounds. Mick the Miller was not the only example of this. Loughnagere broke the West Ham 1,000-yard track record in 1930 in an astonishing 81.16 seconds. This achievement would not be bettered in the following 40-odd years of West Ham greyhound racing and so was destined to stand forever.

For all this, the continuance of the duel role of West Ham greyhounds as racers and coursers together with confirmation of the quality of the track's kennels continued to be celebrated in *Stratford Express* of 6 November 1929:

Greyhound Racing

West Ham Stadium greyhounds distinguished themselves at a coursing meeting held at East Hall, Pagleaham, Essex on Monday. Four West Ham dogs – Horder, Barna Skipper and Poperingbe – entered the second ties. Horder beat Barba Skipper, but Poperingbe lost to Black Letter. In the final ties however, Horder won in excellent style. Horder also won the Kennel Sweepstakes at West Ham Stadium on Saturday.

Edisray, another West Ham dog, won the Crouch Hill Stakes at East Hall. The judge at the previous coursing meeting at which Cosy Como and Farmer Boy, two West Ham dogs, won their deciding ties, made comment on the splendid condition of the dogs from West Ham kennels.

However, Mick the Miller would help place tradition where it belongs and put racing squarely to the fore in terms of greyhound sport. Over 70 years after his legendary exploits in the early era of greyhound racing, 'The Miller' remains more of a household name as any other racing dog and the only greyhound to become a film star. His ancestry can be traced back to Master McGraph, triple Waterloo Cup winner in the nineteenth century. Until recent times his remains stood embalmed at the Natural History Museum in Kensington, London, before being moved to a museum at Tring where he still takes pride of place. His story is one of the most celebrated in the history of greyhound sport, but he was lucky to make it to the racetrack.

Whelped from Na Boc Lei from a mating to Glorious Event, Mick the Miller, the greatest dog to run on the flat, came in the same litter as one of the best ever hurdlers, Macoma. Many believe that his original owner was the parish priest, Father Martin Brophy, his real name was Murphy, but priests were only allowed to be involved with racing dogs under an assumed name. However Mick first belonged to another Irish priest, Father Browne (real name Twyford). Browne was aware of the effect of choosing Na Boc Lei. She was a fine greyhound, perfect for breeding, but her sire was the top coursing dog, Let 'Im Out. This dog had reached the finals of the Irish Cup, the Tipperary Cup, the Cork Cup and the Greenall Cup, on the fuel of his determination and brave running. However, his stamina always seemed to let him down at the last hurdle, but this was probably more to do with his training than his genetic make up. Let 'Im Out was to pass on his courage and fortitude to his grandsons, Mick the Miller and Macoma.

Mick was one of a litter of eleven born in June 1926. At birth he seemed to Browne the weakest of his litter and as such he decided it would be best to send him elsewhere. So Mick went to Brophy's vicarage where he got his name from Mick Miller, who was an odd-job man at the vicarage where the dog was to be raised. One odd-job Miller undertook was the looking after of the canine wizard to be. Shortly before his first birthday, he contracted distemper, a highly contagious viral disease that, in the main, affects dogs. At the time there were no vaccines for this malady and the odds were stacked against his chances of

survival. But Father Brophy refused to give up on his animal and took the dog to vet Arthur Callanan, who was to later become the manager of Shelbourne Park Race Track in Ireland before moving on to Wimbledon.

The Miller was very weak but Callanan considered that there might be a chance of rescuing him. The vet/manager advised the owner to leave the sick young dog with him. Days and nights of struggle followed but the effort paid off when some months later, in a state of growing good health, Mick the Miller was returned to his owner priest with the recommendation to give the lad a long convalescence free from trial running. This is the explanation for the late start to Mick's racing career.

As such, it was not until April 1928 that the 18-month-old Mick The Miller was taken back to Shelbourne Park for his first trials. He was placed with Mick Horan for training. Horan schooled Mick and his brother Macoma over the hurdles, and found that the Miller was as good a jumper as his sibling. Horan was to claim that Mick would have performed equally well if he had contested hurdle events throughout his career. The two dogs were both able to get results anywhere, over all distances and types of racing, however the decision was made to race one on the flat and the other over the jumps.

Mick made his racing debut at Shelbourne Park on 18 April 1928. He won easily and went on to compete in 20 more races in Ireland. He won 15 of these and gained a reputation that depicted him as an awesome racing creature. The last race he lost in Ireland was the final of the Easter Cup in April 1929, when Odd Blade, who had won the inaugural Easter Cup the year before, held him off. At this juncture Horan understood that he had a racing phenomenon on his hands and as such counselled Father Brophy to put his dog in for the English Derby in June.

Mick the Miller landed in Britain in May 1929. In his first trial at White City his time and style of racing impressed the track establishment and the greyhound media, so much so that almost immediately he was made favourite to win the Derby. In those days Britain's premier Classic was restricted to 48 runners and was decided over four races.

Straight after his trial it seemed that everyone wanted to buy Mick the Miller, so Father Brophy auctioned the rising star on the terrace steps of White City. He was sold to Albert H. Williams, a London bookmaker for 800 guineas, an incredible price for a novice in the 1920s, but retrospectively a give-away fee. The drama of this sale caused enough notoriety to make the London evening papers that same day. A greyhound had never cost so much and it was thought that any animal bringing such a sum had to be something special. Father Brophy and Mick Horan went back to Ireland far richer men than the rather strange pairing who had arrived in Britain with hope and a dog.

A massive audience was attracted to Mick the Miller's first race on 16 July, a first-round heat of the 1929 Derby. Not only did he win, he destroyed what was before that race thought to be the unachievable half-minute barrier for the 525 yards at White City. He covered the distance in 29.82 seconds, which was a national record. He smashed through to the second round and semi-finals in a similar fashion and thus came to the final as a hot 7-4 on favourite to land the £700 purse. It was the lowest prize given to a Derby winner, but winning it would come near to paying back his purchase price. However, he was beaten into second place by Palatinus, but the run was declared a no-race and in the re-run 30 minutes later he pulverised Palatinus by three lengths in 29.96 seconds. Mick the Miller had become a celebrity.

A few days after his Derby triumph, Mick was in action again, banging out victory after victory. He won more than £1,200 in prize money in various events and match races before once more being sold, but this time for the massive sum of 2,000 guineas to Mr Arundel Kempton, who gave the dog to his wife as a gift. Thereafter the Miller took up residence at Sidney Orton's kennels at Wimbledon.

Again Mick was rocketed into the headlines. Never before had a dog been sold for more than £1,000 and at a time of deep financial insecurity. With the Wall Street Crash and the start of the Depression just three months off, the Miller came as a welcome distraction to many. He gave greyhound racing a real boost in its early years, bringing excitement and romance to the sport, and this helped establish it in the consciousness of the whole of Britain. His calmness was a great asset to him, but he was thought by many to be the cleverest dog ever to race and he won more by trackcraft than by speed, seemingly knowing that the inside position was the shortest way home. Mick was never over excited in the way that costs so many dogs so much; he was rarely out of the traps like lightning. But this was more of an advantage to him than a problem. When other dogs were booming down the straight to the initial turn, Mick was just off the running, prepared to cut into the rails at the first glimmer of a gap, whilst the faster dogs were running wide. He also had a good reserve of stamina, was able to fight and then come again in his struggles for the rails. He was strongest over 525 yards up to 700 yards, but he was a bit exposed over shorter distances, which is why he never impressed in the Laurels at his home track where he was never to show his best form. He was steered clear of the Gold Collar and the Scurry Cup for similar reasons. Mick preferred the long haul to the sprint. As such he relished White City, Wembley and, in particular, West Ham's long gallop, with its generous turns. His trainer was wise enough to pick and choose his races at these venues.

Following his first Derby victory, the Miller entered the International at West Ham; this was a 600-yard event. Trouncing his rivals by seven lengths in his heat early in the afternoon, in the evening of the same day Mick took the £200 final by four lengths. In November, back at White City in the London Cup, he won his first and second round heats and the semi-final, but he lost the final by a short head. He finished the year by winning his heat and semi-final for the Champion Stakes at Wimbledon over 550 yards, but he was badly baulked again and was only able to take the runners-up spot.

'Bradshaw Fold'

Beware the Hammer dog

As the 1930s started, Mick the Miller was winning race after race. He was back at Wembley in March to win the prestigious Spring Cup, and in June he won the Derby again, going through the event as he did the previous year, unbeaten. No other hound was to win the Derby two years in succession whilst West Ham was operating, although Patricia's Hope did it in 1972 and 1973. Mick had been out of traps 1 and 4 only once in his two wins. He took the title by three lengths from the West Ham bitch Bradshaw Fold, the only animal in 1930 to give him a real challenge on the track.

The brilliant black bitch Bradshaw Fold was one of the few greyhounds to rival Mick the Miller in the early 1930s. Their contests never failed to attract hoards of spectators and punters. Indeed, Mick, who was at the height of his powers, was the only greyhound in Britain able to beat her as the thirties dawned.

Jewel, as those who handled her affectionately called her, was the first truly great racing bitch and one of the most popular greyhounds ever to run at West Ham. Alongside Queen of Suir she was the best-known bitch of her era. Bred in England her confrontations with Mick the Miller had the added spice of being England against Ireland events. She was owned and reared by Mr A.R. Hughes of Manchester who also trained her before Stanley Biss took her on-board.

Stanley Biss began racing by entering a greyhound in co-ownership with Ken Appleton in the first days of the Wembley track. These two men became the most successful West Ham trainers before the Second World War. Biss was the first greyhound trainer to become a household name. He was one of a number of the finest greyhound trainers to be connected with the West Ham track in its early years, but he was certainly the most famous of them, being probably the greatest handler of bitches. No one understood their moods and peak periods of racing better than Biss. On the last day of 1933 he needed Queen of the Suir to win £100 or more for him to become the first trainer to win £10,000 for his owners in one year. The 'Queen' did the business, claiming a first prize of £125, which enabled Stanley Biss to achieve the ambition that was to make him famous throughout Britain.

Biss later moved to Catford where he achieved a similar success, being champion trainer again in 1948 when his dogs won over £20,000 in prize money. But the greatest prize of all, the Derby, always eluded him.

Bradshaw Fold was whelped in 1928. Her sire was Newville Captain. Her dam, December Girl, was something of a waif and stray. She never raced and had spent part of her life roaming the highways and byways of Manchester. Like Mick the Miller, Jewel was a game and intelligent animal and it was these qualities that made her so popular with the track faithful. It was probably with her that the association between black bitches and staying power began; others with similar qualities included Disputed Rattler, Unwin Beauty and Dolores Rocket. In March 1930 she ran West Ham's 700-yard circuit in 40.04 seconds. This stood as a track and world record for nearly two decades when Lilac's Luck became the first to smash the 40-second barrier, covering the distance in 39.88 seconds. However, the West Ham ring had been much improved by that time.

Bradshaw Fold won the Coronation Stakes at Wembley, her favorite track, in 1931 in a time of 30.5 seconds. She followed this performance with another Wembley final appearance in October, this time in the St Leger, but although she ran as the bitch of genius she was, Mick the Miller once again bettered her. This was to be her final race and at the end of the year she retired and spent her last days with her owner, sleeping in his bedroom. She was hardly ever parted from him until she passed away in 1939.

Bradshaw Fold was one of the first true stars of the early days of greyhound racing, moving to the far reaches of the nation's then extensive railway network to contest open events, often arriving only just before her race, but always enthusiastic and eager to compete she was a true canine Hammer.

More Mick Classics

Only two days after the Derby, Mick the Miller was at West Ham for the 1930 Cesarewitch, run that year over 600 yards. He was not to taste defeat from heats to final. Twice he set national records for the course, clocking 34.01 seconds in his semi-final. In July Mick took the Welsh Derby at the White City, Cardiff (not a Classic at that time) in similar fashion, setting a national record of 29.55 seconds in the final, beating his own national record set the week before when romping home in his first heat. In a period of six weeks he had set four national and world records for 600 yards and 525 yards. Constant racing eventually caught up with Mick however and he was eliminated in the first round of the Laurels at Wimbledon the following month, finishing sixth in his heat.

Mick the Miller was then rested and he did not appear in competitive action again until the spring of 1931. In March he went through the Spring Cup at Wembley unbeaten; his time of 30.04 seconds in the final was a track record. In less than two years, from his initial race in Britain to 16 May 1931, when he was victorious in an open race at White City, he was involved in twenty-five contests and nine match races. Only five times was he denied first place, but he was runner-up in four of these by either a short head or a neck. At one point he won nine races in succession. As such, Mick was a powerful entry in his third Derby.

Seldom Led was seldom led

This was the first Derby that was affected by allegations that a dog had been poisoned. After the first round there was the surprising defeat of Maiden's Boy, who had been hotly fancied, having a reputation as something of a stayer. The 7-4 favourite finished last and looked exhausted. S. Young, his owner/trainer wrote of his surprise in a letter to the *Greyhound Mirror and Gazette*, that their correspondent had failed to be informed before the race that Maiden's Boy was unfit. He told how he had let people know that it would be unwise to chance money on the animal. Young explained:

> The dog was never in better health than when we left him at the kennel on Saturday evening, and we had no qualms about his safety and perfect condition when we made our way to White City to see the Mick the Miller – Doumergue match … When my head kennel lad went to take Maiden's Boy for his customary stroll, the dog was tottering on his feet and looked very bad.

Professor McCunn, a leading vet, was asked to look at the greyhound and he stayed with the dog and Young all through Sunday night. As Monday morning dawned Maiden's Boy was still sick, but looked to have improved. McCann let Young know that his dog was a fighter and that he might be able to run on the Tuesday evening. Young elaborated:

> I was loath to run the dog in that condition … But I realised that hundreds of people had backed him to win the Derby and that the sheer determination and pluck of the dog might help him gain second place and thereby qualify.

He went on to express his confidence that Maiden's Boy could have won the Derby and put up £100 to match the eventual winner. Young declared,

> I am not crying because my dog was beaten. I only want the public to know the truth.

Ryland R, a huge Irish dog who tipped the scales at 80 pounds, broke the track record at White City beating Mick the Miller in the second round with a fantastic 29.69 second run. The *Greyhound Mirror and Gazette* proclaimed him the most wonderful greyhound the sport has produced. In the week before the finals Reginald Haswell, the tipster for the *Greyhound Mirror*, gave an entire page to the beast, telling of its qualities, forecasting great things for

Seldom Led

the two-and-a-quarter year old that had developed with every run. However, in the second round there was some panic with the news that Ryland R had sprung a toe. Arthur 'Doc' Callanan, his trainer, the same man who had nursed Mick the Miller as a pup, toiled swiftly to ready the hound for the semi-final, where, ironically, Ryland at 5-4 met 'The Miller', a 2-1 shot for the race. Ryland R led from the start, leaving Mick trailing the field. But MM wasn't finished, running with speed and guile to challenge Ryland R at the line, but the big dog won by just half a length.

Ryland R was back to his best following the seven days of rest between the semi and the final, his owner telling how,

> The swelling has subsided, and I think that Ryland R will win. If he should be defeated, no fault will be attached to the toe injury. He seems ready for the fray, and if he is beaten, it will be because the better dog had beaten him.

Although Ryland R had taken the media spotlight away from Mick the Miller, Sydney Orton was predicting that his student would become a three-time Derby winner, saying,

> I am very, very hopeful ... Mick has given me every satisfaction, and I have him as fit as when he won his first Derby. His shoulder injury is completely cured, and there is no sign of it returning. Mick will win this year's Derby if he escapes bumping and boring. Yes, I am exceedingly confident and am not much scared of the opposition.

Also in the final six were Brunswick Bill, Seldom Led, Golden Hammer and Mick's Fancy. Golden Hammer had cost his owner just £2, but Jim Snyder, his trainer, was optimistic following his dog's placement in trap 1. Seldom Led, a West Ham trained dog, who had been bought for a five pound note, had not been so fortunate, having been drawn in trap 4. A. Green saw his trainee as still on the way to his best, but as having a decent chance in the race, he argued 'It is very likely Seldom Led will live up to his name.'

In the first round Brunswick Bill had led from the start, having grabbed the rails and covered the course in 30 seconds, thereby making the fastest time at White City that year and defeating Seldom Led by five lengths. Mick's Fancy was in trap 3. He had beaten Mick the Miller home in the first round. In heat eleven Mick had come into the betting at 5-1 on. However, a lot of money went on Mick's Fancy, drawing the Miller back to 7-2 on at the start of the race. Mick was drawn on the rails, his favourite station, and he got out well, leading the field at the first turn, but following a general cluster Mick the Miller and Bright Cheer broke free. At bend four Bright Cheer began to look drained and the Miller looked home and dry, but from nowhere Mick's Fancy hit the gas to belt over the line to take the race by one-and-a-half lengths from Mick the Miller, who had O'Brazil just half a length behind him (the latter animal might have taken the race had he avoided a bump at the first bend). A winning time of 30.66 seconds was not a fast time, but it was enough. It was reported that after this race a £1,200 offer for Mick's Fancy was made and refused.

Seventy thousand people attended the 1931, £1,050, English Derby final at White City. At 9 p.m. they made a sound that was 'reminiscent of an English Cup final' according to Reginald Haswell in the *Greyhound Mirror*.

Mick the Miller had made his third final but he did not do it in the style to which his supporters had become accustomed. Time, it seemed, was taking its toll on the Miller. At the first bend Ryland R was just in front, moving easily over the ground like the natural athlete he was, eating up the track with his huge, gorging strides. Mick the Miller had got off to a poor start and with half the course to go he was at the back of the field. Ryland R was still in charge at the home turn but at that point Seldom Led drew on his reserves and came alongside the Irish giant. This seemed to surprise and even unnerve Ryland, who noticeably tired as the West Ham dog appeared. The two dogs swung wide on the bend and the collective sense of the massive audience became tangible, the expectation was that the Miller was working things out, having ducked and dived his way to third place. They began to bring him home on a wave of enthusiasm. But Golden Hammer, who had been holding the rails, had other ideas and began to fight the most cunning hound who ever breathed with sheer animal resistance. They zoomed past the finishing post as one, but Mick had taken it by a head. The stadium was filled with the noise that only comes of the merging of celebration and exhilaration, but the sound fell away like a stone when it was noted that a red light had cut through the dusky evening telling the world that a 'no race' had been run.

The bend stewards accused Ryland R of assaulting a fellow runner whilst it was challenging for a place. The GRA men had reported this and the red light had been illuminated and a klaxon sounded (useless in the sea of sound created by the crowd) before the mighty Mick had come home. The disapproval of the great punting horde was quickly made obvious as the grand White City was transformed into a cauldron of boos.

Maybe Ryland R's mistake could have been put down to his injury, but the

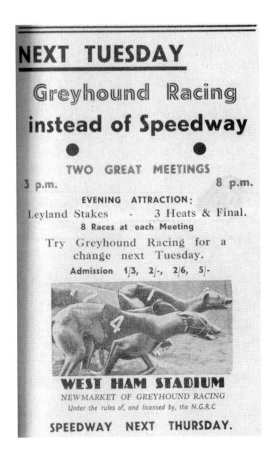

NEXT TUESDAY

Greyhound Racing instead of Speedway

● ●

TWO GREAT MEETINGS

3 p.m.   8 p.m.

EVENING ATTRACTION:

Leyland Stakes - 3 Heats & Final.

8 Races at each Meeting

Try Greyhound Racing for a change next Tuesday.

Admission 1/3, 2/-, 2/6, 5/-

WEST HAM STADIUM

NEWMARKET OF GREYHOUND RACING

Under the rules of, and licensed by, the N.G.R.C

SPEEDWAY NEXT THURSDAY.

fact that he had moved wide meant that he had effected Seldom Led detrimentally. As in his first Derby, Mick would have to 'go again'. With Ryland R disqualified, the five remaining dogs came back to the traps thirty minutes later. Mick the Miller started off in the betting at 4-5 but eased to evens favourite by the off. The re-run was something of a let-down compared with the first attempt to find a Derby Champion for 1931. Golden Hammer, Seldom Led and Brunswick Bill came out together, but it was Golden Hammer who claimed the rails and took the initial bend first. However, by the next bend Seldom Led was in front and he didn't let go, coming home a winner by four lengths. Golden Hammer who claimed the £300 second prize followed him in. Mick's Fancy beat a tired Mick the Miller who could do no better than fourth.

Seldom Led, an exceptionally good-looking animal, was blessed with speed and the stamina that enabled him to take the re-run of the Derby. He was the first and last West Ham trained dog to win the English Greyhound Derby, but the Premier Greyhound event of 1931 had been won by the best dog of the year. He covered the 525 yards in 30.04 seconds. In his racing career Seldom Led competed in 62 races and won 31 of them. He took a score of trophies over every distance up to 700 yards and all types of track. His triumphs included the

Trafalgar Cup and the Christmas Cup at Wembley, where he held the 700-yard record of 40.72 seconds. After the Derby his owner, Mr J.J. Flemming, was to move him to Wimbledon under trainer J. Hannafin.

SELDOM LED			April 1929 Fawn Dog
Society Boy	Silver Spoon	Heart of Oak Again	
		Atlantic Flight	
	Silent One	Commandant Pearse	
		Scalaway	
Pity	The Tetrarch II	The Monarch	
		Start in Time	
	Marks of Misfortune	Lord Londonderry	
		Maids of Misfortune	

Mick returns

Mick the Miller was again to contest the Cesarewitch and the Welsh Derby, but without success. The St Leger, run on 3 October 1931, over a course the length of which was outside his experience, was to be his last major race. He was now over five years old and many thought the task was beyond him. However Mick loved to race and he fought as if he knew it was his swansong. He came home the winner, by a length from Virile Bill, to the rapturous cheers of the huge Wembley crowd. Yet again he had not allowed himself to be beaten in a major event. In his Classic victories he had remained unbeaten, a record without parallel.

His racing days were done, but Mick The Miller stayed very much in the limelight. After a couple of years at stud he took the leading role in a 1935 Gainsborough film based on his own career, entitled *Wild Boy*. He was reputed to be a very intelligent animal and he was a natural for the part. After his days of stardom, he made the occasional stage appearance for charity, and turned out for personal appearances to open new greyhound tracks.

Virile Bill

Mick the Miller visits the famous steeplechaser Golden Miller following
Mick the Miller's 1931 St Leger victory

Mick the Miller's racing record

Country	Number of races	Wins	Seconds
Ireland	20	15	3
England	61	46	10
Total	81	61	13

As can be seen from the above table, Mick the Miller was only out of the first two on seven occasions in his entire racing career. Much of this was due to his intelligence. He seemed to know how to conserve his strength and fitness, always slowing down immediately he knew he had passed the finishing line. A 50 guinea stud animal, he failed to match the success of his brother Macoma, but in his defence it must be pointed out that he served a number of bitches that had no track experience. His best sons included Glen Ranger and Mick the Moocher. Gallant Ruth, the 1934 Oaks winner, and Greta's Rosary (from a mating with the Derby champion Greta Ranee, the first bitch to win the event) were his daughters. The latter followed her sire by winning the 1938 St Leger.

MICK THE MILLER		June 1926 brindled dog
Glorious Event	Osprey Hawk	Hillcourt Prairie Hawk
	Merriment IV	Dick the Liar Royal Leily
Na Boc Lei	Let 'in Out	Lock And Key Lengsfield
	Talbotstown III	Coming Tide Bag O'Slack

Mick The Miller gave a tremendous boost to greyhound racing. At the zenith of his reign as a racer near to 20 million people were attending 220 tracks in Britain (many of them flappers). He died a legend in his own lifetime on 5 May 1939 at the age of 13. After his death his heart was weighed and was 1.5 ounces heavier than the average racing greyhound. The publicity he received when the sport was young did much to establish the tradition and reputation of Irish breeders. He was the dog who 'made' greyhound racing; his personality and brilliance on the track were a major force in popularising the new spectator sport in England.

> A magpie, a humbug, striped Geordie so fast,
> Hugging the fence, the six dog flashes past,
> Rapid insider, rushing strider,
> Now he's up close beside yer,
> Looking for that flashing, twinkling slit of hope,
> Like that thieving bird, he runs a slippery slope,
> But if he can hold the tight, unforgiving turn,
> The prize, the trophy, the respect he will earn.

From '*The Ballad of the West Ham Dogs*'

You will know them by their colours

5
THE CUTLET, THE QUEEN AND BOB

Future Cutlet

Having failed to get any serious promises of support from the coursing fraternity, the Association, as the track at Manchester approached completion, bought greyhounds themselves, giving some away to suitable people and running others. In a short time, however, after a beginning had been made, seeing the allurements of the sport, and the overwhelming public interest that was manifest, outsiders expressed their desire to enter dogs, and before long there was a waiting list of private owners.

Croxton Smith, A. (1927) *Greyhound Racing and Breeding*.

Gay and Hancock Ltd, London

Going to the dogs

People are connected closely to greyhound racing by a limited number of ties. Human relationships to racing dogs tend to be restricted within the interaction that takes place between the greyhounds and their handlers, trainers, owners and the type of punters who attended West Ham greyhound meetings. Some people take more than one role. A few fulfil all these functions. However, all those involved with greyhound sport have an association with the seven imponderables of human existence: fate, destiny, fortune, chance, providence and perhaps ultimately doom. As such, they 'walk on the wild side' more or less – that is the fee for excitement. Once in these eddies of life one is bound to them as they provide a kind of 'high', constantly creating or fulfilling desires, wishes and dreams, at the same time thwarting ambitions, aims and hopes. This is a maelstrom of unpredictability that mirrors life if it is led in anything like an active way; in fact, the entire experience that is greyhound racing emphasises the processes of life. The encounter with the track obliges us to live with the fickle, the unknown, and to use what one can to control the variables.

This may be the central appeal of sports like greyhound racing: the feeling that we, as human beings, might have some say in or control over the vagaries of nature, exemplified in the dogs. Herein is the central focus of greyhound racing – its restless core of tension. It enables us to think we might train the course of the future and make it run in accordance with our desires. In this way we fire the belief we can find and tap the conduits or channel the very forces that drive our mortality and the universe itself in our favour. The whole regime is one of totem and taboo ground into 'form', honed out of breeding, training and diet set in the predictable rhythms of repetition. The season, the structure of the meetings, delivered in time over preordained distances are our means to corral the inextricable and ineffable powers that seem to impinge on our every move. Regulations, rules and laws are deployed to harness the chaotic spirits that threaten to overwhelm us. The unpredictable, the tangential, the tenuous, the intangible are locked within the predictable, material world. The wispy spectre of possibility is charmed into the realms of probability, by use of clock, the judge, handicaps, traps, and odds. Our faith is derived from arithmetic and mathematics. These mechanisms are facets of an entire institution, the track and its forebears of the racecourse and the coursing field. These milieux were themselves rooted at the dawn of humanity in the rituals of prehistoric nature religions and rites of passage, retranslated and transplanted at the very beginnings of the industrial era via military influences and aristocratic traditions.

As such, the story of West Ham greyhound racing is much more than a history of dogs, their races, triumphs and disasters, but what we can tell is wound up in these tales of lineage and career. The phantom of everything that drove people to 'go to the dogs' at West Ham is captured between the lines of the 'facts and figures', which include a love of and fidelity to a place. Custom House stadium cradled the pumping heart of life that was epitomised in the tens of thousands of acts that brought any greyhound to the East End, made their events and their races possible, and their history, their existence, happen.

Future Cutlet, a dog with a past

Future Cutlet was in every sense a champion dog. This brindle by Mutton Cutlet out of Wary Guide was whelped in April 1929. His sire was a dark brindle by Jamie out of Miss Cinderella. He was born and raised at Major McCalmont's famous Cotswold kennels. Whelped in March 1921, Mutton Cutlet contested the Waterloo Cup in 1923, 1924 and 1925. He was swift and brave, but failed to reach a final, although he ran up for the Waterloo Plate in 1924. In 1926, he was brought by Tom Morris, keeper of the Irish Stud book, and put to stud in Ireland at a fee of 10 guineas. During the first two or three years he served only a small number of bitches, but by the time he died in November 1934 he had sired 522 winners on the track and coursing field.

Mutton Cutlet was the sire of, among others, Valiant Cutlet, Beef Cutlet and Mr Moon, each of them an important sire in their own right. Beef Cutlet was the sire of the fine Junior Classic and Juvenile Classic, Loose Lead and Laird's Cutlet, while Mr Moon was the sire of the great Ballynennan Moon. These were all outstanding greyhounds.

Future Cutlet was another of Mutton Cutlet's first-class sons. Although his sire was English, Future Cutlet was born and bred in Ireland. He was purchased for £600, a very large sum in 1930, by W.A. Evershed to race at the newly opened Wembley Stadium track. He was trained by Sidney Probert and entered for the 1931 Laurels, which he won in 28.52 seconds – considered fast at that time. The young dog was then two years old and it was decided that his Derby entry should be delayed until the following year. He was, however, entered for the Cesarewitch over 600 yards at West Ham, and on his way to taking the trophy he set a new national record for the 600-yard course in his heat. This was the year Custom House stadium, which had a number of owners throughout its history, came under the umbrella of Wembley Stadium Ltd.

So, Future Cutlet had won two Classics by the time he was two-and-a-half years old. And the best was still to come. In 1932 he ran to victory in Wembley's Spring Cup and, in spite of his early successes, odds of 100-1 were quoted against his winning the Derby, but he went close to proving the bookmakers totally wrong. In the final, he met the northern flier Wild Woolley. From the time the dogs sprang out of the traps, the race was between the two star animals. Wild Woolley just managed to grab the verdict by a neck, the pair having crossed the winning line together ten lengths in front of the also-rans.

When winning his heat for the 1932 Derby, Future Cutlet set a new track record at White City with a time of 29.62 seconds for the 525-yard course. He also held the record for Wembley over the same distance. In the 1932 Cesarewitch he set a new world record of 33.78 seconds in his semi-final before running to his third Classic triumph and becoming the only greyhound to win the West Ham Cesarewitch twice.

God save the Queen

Stanley Biss took the West Ham bitch Queen of the Suir to two successive Oakes in 1932 and 1933. The race is confined to bitches and was first contested in 1927, so alongside the Derby it is the oldest Classic.

Until 1958 the Oaks was run at White City; the event was thereafter transferred to Harringay. The first Oaks was run over 500 yards and was won by Three of Spades, who was trained at Harringay by Sid Jennings.

The Queen achieved her first Oaks win in a time of 30.89 seconds, but she bettered this the following year with a run of 30.23 seconds. She was by Mutton Cutlet out of the Melksham Tom bitch Burette. Queen of Suir was whelped in

Bella

May 1930 and came from one of the greatest litters of all time, which included Beef Cutlet and the bitch Bella. For three years, from early 1932 until the end of 1934, the Queen completely dominated she-dog events. Her grand sires Jamie and Melksham Tom not only produced the finest coursing stock of the time but also the best racing greyhounds. Melksham Tom was to sire Other Days, sire of Brilliant Bob and the bitch Banriogan Dann, dam of Ballynennan Moon from a mating with Mutton Cutlet's son Mr Moon. Many of the finest performers during the first twenty years of the sport were of this breeding. It was the solid foundation on which greyhound racing developed in the British Isles and in America, combining speed, stamina, track sense and courage, the attributes of top-quality greyhounds.

Queen of the Suir's litter was bred and reared by Mr J.A. Byrne of Co. Tipperary. After selling Beef Cutlet he retained Bella and Queen of Suir as he hoped to breed from them if they proved a success on the track. Queen of Suir was entered for the first Irish Oaks at Clonmel in 1932, the only time it was run over 550 yards. She won convincingly from Silvery Sail and it was decided to place her with Stanley Biss, in preparation for the English Oaks. Her win in the Classic made her the first and only bitch to win both the English and Irish Oaks.

After her seasonal rest she was entered for the 1933 Coronation Stakes, an event for bitches at Wembley, which she won in the fast time of 30.06 seconds. She was again entered for the Oaks, which she ran with greater brilliance than the year before to make it two in a row, an achievement equalled only by Ballinasloe Blonde in 1961 and 1962 and Cranog Bet in 1963 and 1964 in the West Ham era. However, with her win in Ireland Queen of Suir was now a triple Oaks winner, something no other bitch accomplished whilst Custom House was hosting greyhound meetings.

The Queen was off racing throughout the winter of 1933 but came back in February 1934, when almost four years old, and once more won the Coronation Stakes, the most important event for bitches after the Oaks. Her time of 30.03 seconds was equalled only by Quarter Day four years later, who set a new record the following year when she too won for a second time.

Queen of the Suir

The Queen also raced at Wimbledon, Harringay, Catford, Southend and Belle Vue Manchester and won a number of other top titles, including the Orient Cup and the London Cup at Clapton, establishing a track record for the 550-yard course. In her three years' running, contesting only a few top events, Queen of the Suir won more than £2,000. After being served by a number of important sires and producing little of note she was put to Maiden's Boy, twice winner of the Wembley Gold Cup and the St Leger in 1930. She was nine years old and Maiden's Boy was almost eleven when in 1939 she whelped Brave Damsel. She won the Irish Derby in 1941, becoming one of the few bitches to take the Shelbourne Park Classic, beating another bitch, She's Tidy, into second place. It was The Queen of Suir's last litter but she had proved herself both on and off the track.

QUEEN OF SUIR		June 1930 brindled bitch
Mutton Cutlet	Jamie	Beaded Brow
		Jibstay
	Miss Cinderella	Rathaldron
		Rosta
Burette	Melksham Tom	Staff Officer
		Melksham Nellie
	Rigadoon	?
		?

Future was bright

By the time Future Cutlet challenged for the 1933 Derby, he was four years and three months old. Wild Woolley was again taking part, together with Beef Cutlet, who was running brilliantly. Given the competition, most aficionados

FUTURE CUTLET		April 1929 brindled dog
Mutton Cutlet	Jamie	Beaded Brow Jibstay
	Miss Cinderella	Rathaldron Rosta
Wary Guide	Guiding Hand	Irish Steeple Fashion Plate
	Wireless Waves	Three Speed Cara Dilis

gave Future Cutlet little chance. But, as was his wont, he ran out of his skin, hitting the finish almost joined to Beef Cutlet. He took the race by a neck and became the oldest dog ever to win the Derby. Later that year, in the Wimbledon Champion Stakes, it was Beef Cutlet who got the verdict by a short head, but there was very little light between them.

At the end of that summer Future Cutlet retired. Mr Evershed had set up a trust fund for his champion so that he would live well for what remained of his days. According to Sidney Probert he was a highly strung dog, difficult to train, but Future Cutlet was only once unplaced during his entire career. He was probably the fastest trapper before Ballyhennessy Seal.

Captain Brice, the racing manager at Wembley in the late 1920s-1930s, described Future Cutlet as 'the best looker of them all'. He was certainly a beautifully proportioned dog, which always gave a stylish performance. His four English Classic wins were achieved over a period of three years; at that point, no other greyhound had then ever achieved that feat over so long a period.

The roaring thirties

A total of 20,176,260 tickets to see the dogs were sold in 1932. In 1933 Longfellow II took the West Ham track record for the 600-yard hurdles in a time of 34.94 seconds. This fawn dog, by Main Guard and Ardmore Belle, was whelped in July 1930. He was owned by Miss H. Potter and was another Orton trained animal based at Wimbledon. At one time he was the holder of three national hurdles records, the 600 yards (34.94 seconds) and the 550 yards (31.77 seconds), both established at West Ham, and the 500 yards (29.24 seconds) achieved at Wimbledon. On 20 May 1933 Longfellow II won the Midland Hurdles Championship. He was also to take the Autumn Stakes and was a semi-finalist in both the Christmas Vase at Wimbledon and the National Open Hurdles at Clapton in the same year.

Elsell was the 1933 Cesarewitch victor in 34.22 seconds. However, 1934 saw the race go to one of the most wonderful dogs ever to run at Custom House. Mr Billy Quinn bred Brilliant Bob in Co. Tipperary, Ireland. Later he bred and owned the impressive and influential Quare Times.

When Brilliant Bob was a puppy Mr Quinn sold a half share of the dog to an Irish farmer, but they were persuaded to part with him, by Wimbledon trainer Sidney Orton, who knew of the Bob's capabilities and had recommended him to his patron, Mr A.J. Dearman.

By Other Ways out of Birchfield Bessie and whelped in 1931, Brilliant Bob was aptly named, as he was one of the best track and coursing field dogs in the history of greyhound sport. He first made the greyhound world sit up and take notice in 1933, when, as a puppy, he won Ireland's oldest coursing event, the Tipperary Cup. He was introduced to track racing in the spring of that year and he finished runner-up in the Easter Cup. Later that year Bob demonstrated his tremendous early pace, but also showed that he possessed the stamina for long distances when winning the 1933 Irish St Leger, the only time it was run at Clonmel, in a time of 31.53 seconds.

After resting through the winter, BB was ready to again contest the Easter Cup in the spring of 1934. On this occasion he made quite sure, winning in a fast time of 30.29 seconds. The superb Monarch of the Glen could do no better, clocking 30.43 seconds to win the event a decade later.

It was at this stage in his career that Bob's owners let their champion go, having already proved himself as a dual-purpose dog of brilliance. He was sold for £2,000, a large sum seventy years ago. He arrived in Britain in May, in time to enter the 1934 Laurels at Wimbledon, his new home track. On his arrival BB's trainer saw him as a moody and off-colour dog, so he decided not to train him at all. Instead he let Bob rest and wander about the kennels until he felt more at home.

The trainer's instinct paid off. Brilliant Bob won the Laurels and went on to victory in two other Classics in the same year, a feat never before accomplished. After his first Classic win Bob was entered for the Derby. He got to the final in style, in spite of drawing trap one – not his favourite starting block. In the final he ran into difficulties on the first bend and could do no better than fourth, beaten by the three best greyhounds of the year after himself: Davesland, Grey Raca and Wild Woolley.

In the Scurry Gold Cup at Clapton Brilliant Bob soon made up for his Derby performance. He won his heat and beat the winner of previous year, Creamery Border, in the final. He clocked 23.47 seconds for the 400-yard course, a more than useful time.

In October he took on the Cesarewitch at West Ham. For BB the Custom House track was a totally new experience, its long straights and wide bends were a stark contrast to the Clapton track that was almost circular and relatively small. But shape, size or distance did not intimidate Bob. He was the kind of dog that would take on anything and everything. He won the event in 33.8 seconds, the fastest time recorded when the race was run over 600 yards, a time which was not beaten for the 600-yard course until Prionsa Luath ran 33.77 seconds seventeen years later. This was his third Classic in 1934 and he had also won the St Leger and Easter Cup in Ireland in 1933. He was then only the second greyhound to have won a Classic in England and Ireland, the West Ham dog, Queen of the Suir having been the first.

Brilliant Bob was retired to stud at the end of 1934. The lad was to prove himself as effective in this role as he was in his racing days, siring stock of the highest quality. Monalia Bob and Lawless Bob were two of his best sons but the bitches he produced were to have the biggest impact on the sport, these included Miss McCloud, dam of Lost Light, winner of the 1942 Irish Coursing Derby; Brilliant Moon, dam of the 1939 International Cup winner, Wireless Rally; Really Brilliant, dam of the 1945 Tipperary Cup winner, Rathelogheen Dancer; and Brilliant Gay, dam of Hurry Kitty, who followed her maternal grand sire by winning the 1945 Cesarewitch. Brilliant Gay was a blue brindle and had run up for the Irish Coursing Oaks in 1941. Mated to Castledown Lad at the start of 1943, she was to whelp Paddy the Champion, who was to pass on Brilliant Bob's amazing speed to Astra's Son from his mating to Astra. Astra's Son was to transmit the gift of his parents and grandparents to Prairie Vixen, who from a mating with The Grand Champion (sired by Astra's litter brother, Mad Tanist) was sire of Prairie Peg, the 1955 Irish Oaks winner who, when mated to Hi There, was dam of Prairie Flash, one of the greatest post-war sires.

But it was from the mating of Prairie Peg to Champion Prince (Belia's Prince by Castledown Lad) that produced Pigalle Wonder, the English Derby champion, that we see the influence of Brilliant Bob yet again carried through the dam. Pigalle Wonder, when mated to Rather Fancy, produced Yurituni, a bitch who from a mating to Monalee Champion produced Sole Aim, sire of Columbcille Aim, dam of the 1979 Irish Derby winner, the bitch Penny County. Again on the dam's side Prairie Flash, when mated with Yanka Boy gave Itsastar, the bitch who was to whelp the 1979 Irish Oaks winner, Nameless Pixie. As such, track champions down the years have been bred through the impact of the bitches BB produced and in turn through Pigalle Wonder.

Brilliant Bob's sire Other Days (by Melksham Tom) was also the sire of the oddly named Banriogan Dann, who was the mother of Ballynennan Moon. This being the case, even before Bob was born the influence of his sire and of Melksham Tom was via the dam line. As such, Other Days was sire and grandsire of two of the finest dogs in the history of greyhound sport.

The influence of Brilliant Bob over nearly half a century

Brilliant Bob (1931)

X Civil (B)
|
Brilliant Gay (B)

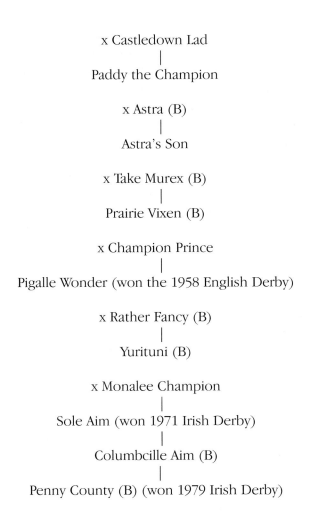

x Castledown Lad
|
Paddy the Champion

x Astra (B)
|
Astra's Son

x Take Murex (B)
|
Prairie Vixen (B)

x Champion Prince
|
Pigalle Wonder (won the 1958 English Derby)

x Rather Fancy (B)
|
Yurituni (B)

x Monalee Champion
|
Sole Aim (won 1971 Irish Derby)
|
Columbcille Aim (B)
|
Penny County (B) (won 1979 Irish Derby)

BRILLIANT BOB		May 1931 fawn & brindled bitch
Mutton Cutlet	Melksham Tom	Staff Officer Melksham Nellie
	Na Boc E	Dick the Liar Coolkeragh
Birchfield Betty	Beaded Dick	Hopsack Beaded Lil
	Ceoil	Osprey Hawk Sweet Cherry

Of all England's great Classics the Derby is King,
And of each of its winners praises we should sing,
But there is one we must forever keep in our head,
And that is the 1931 victor, West Ham's Seldom Led.

Now all thought Mick had won it with poise and grace,
But the Irish Dog Ryland R made it a 'no-race',
And after the re-run, such an exciting thriller,
We saw that Green's dog had defeated the Miller.

Golden Hammer was second to our wonderful hound,
And we'll welcome him back to his cockney home ground,
Knowing behind all the celebration and fuss,
Seldom Led is the only golden Hammer for us.

From '*The Ballad of the West Ham Dogs*'

THROUGHOUT
SEPTEMBER
GREYHOUND RACING

will take place every

MONDAY at 8 p.m.

8 Races

Win & Place & Forecast
Totalisators

Every Comfort & Convenience

(Licenced by, and Racing under the
Rules of, the National Greyhound
Racing Club)

WEST HAM

RACING
EVERY MONDAY
at 8 p.m.

THE WORLD'S FINEST
GREYHOUND RACING

on ENGLAND'S FASTEST TRACK

Win—Place and Forecast Totalisator

WEST HAM
STADIUM

The world's finest and fastest.

6
CALL ME ATAXY!

Naughty Jack Horner

Greyhound racing tracks have been described as the poor man's racecourse, but they are more than that. Among the 330,000 odd who paid for admission in the eleven weeks of racing at Manchester, in 1926, was a considerable proportion of the wealthier classes, and any amount of prominent society women, from duchesses downwards, were running dogs.

Croxton Smith, A. (1927) *Greyhound Racing and Breeding.*
Gay and Hancock Ltd., London

The Betting and Lotteries Act of 1934 changed the entire face of greyhound racing. For the first time it recognised the sport and its tote and extended the powers of the Racecourse Control Board to cover greyhound racing. The tracks were allowed to set up a tote to retain six per cent of its takings for their profit and expense. Under the 1934 Act it was stipulated that:

Betting by way of bookmaking or of totalizer shall not take place . . . in connection with more than eight races . . . during one continuous period not exceeding four hours . . .

I remember a Grand Flight

George Hart, a lifelong follower of greyhound racing and a regular visitor to West Ham from the early thirties to the late sixties, was one of the few people left at the turn of the twenty-first century to have a memory of the 1935 Cesarewitch. Although 86 years old when interviewed about the race, he had a clear memory of the facts:

Grand Flight II was a George Flintham dog. He was fawn, like his mum –
Little Fawn Biddy her name was. He was by Naughty Jack Horner. It won
the final in a good time. Just under 34 seconds I think it was. It beat a
couple of lovely greyhounds, Shove Ha'penny and Ataxy. He'd [Ataxy] got
the West Ham track record for 600 yards the same year. He done that in
33.5 seconds, which was a marvellous run. He'd started the final as 9-2
favourite as he'd beaten Grand Flight in a heat. Ataxy was probably the
faster dog but he was always likely run into trouble, whereas Grand Flight
was a clever dog, a bit like Mick the Miller. Anyway, Grand Flight won the
Cesarewitch in 1935. He won the International that same year, and in the
first part of the Pall Mall, run at Harringay, Grand Flight was only just beat,
by a head, by Shove Ha'penny – they were always to-ing and fro-ing. In
1936 he reached the final of the Derby, but was well out of it in fifth, that
was when Fine Jubilee won it. But he put up a real fight at the White City
to beat Ataxy when he won the *Daily Mirror* Trophy over 725 yards. After
that he went out to stud. He was an honest dog he was. He was one of
Flintham's first dogs and one of his best. Value for money he was, always
put up a good show. He didn't race for long but he did enough to show he
had a lot of character. He was a very popular animal round the tracks.

Lightning dog

Ataxy won the 1936 Cesarewitch in a time of 31.24 seconds. This brindle son of
the black Inler out of Gosher Bead was whelped in 1933, and though not
endowed with the same gift or track sense as many champions, he was still one
of the fastest greyhounds to tread the earth. His sire Inler came to Britain in
1930. Kennelled at Clapton, Inler was a veritable lightning dog out of the traps,
a trait he was to pass on to his sons Tanist and Ataxy. But like so many other
swift dogs, this family tended to hit the first bend at such velocity that it was
sometimes impossible for them to clear it without going wide. This gave slower
animals the chance to move inside them, cutting their journey while the fliers
extended the course. Railers, such as Monday's News and Mick the Miller,
would invariably defeat faster dogs that were unable to take advantage of the
track or race situation. Ataxy was particularly prone to this problem and was
often defeated by slower creatures.

Ataxy came to Britain in 1935 and made his competitive debut at Stamford
Bridge. His fleet footedness convinced his owner, C.C. Keen, to put the puppy
with Leslie Reynolds, who at that time was training out of White City. His first
race there was in the opening round heats of the 1935 Derby in which he beat
the Scurry Cup victor Jack's Joke. In his second round race he experienced a
range of difficulties and went out of the event. But less than a week later in
August he broke two of the White City's most enduring records, the 550-yard,
which he ate up in 30.97 seconds and then the 525-yard, which covered that
distance in 29.56 seconds. No dog had ever held the two records at the same

time. He was immediately made favourite to win the West Ham Cesarewitch. In his first round heat, running at 6-1 on, he caused a real shock by defeating the gargantuan Brilliant Bob by no less than twelve lengths. In the second round he beat Bosham, a St Leger winner, by almost the same margin, taking the track record on the way, running 33.67 seconds for the course. The semi-final put him up against Mr Flintham's greyhound Grand Flight II, which he duly brushed aside with a winning gap of eight lengths in a new world record time of 33.5 seconds, nine lengths ahead of the time set by Mick the Miller half a decade earlier.

Given this record, it is perhaps not surprising that Ataxy was made odds-on favourite for the title, but he had a race fraught with difficulties and could only make fourth place behind Grand Flight II, who ran the course in 33.97 seconds. It was a disappointing anti-climax given the form he had shown up to the final.

It began to seem that Ataxy would be an underachiever always denied a Classic win. He appeared to totally go to pieces in finals. However, in the Wembley St Leger of 1936 he managed to hold things together and live up to his potential. He won his heat and semi-final despite getting severe bumpings all the way round and coming down the straight on each occasion well behind the rest of the dogs. It was only his phenomenal pace over the final few yards that pulled him through. Shove Ha'penny was waiting for him in the final but he blew his rival away, setting new national, Wembley and St Leger records into the bargain, clocking 40.39 seconds. The time was to be unbeaten for almost a decade.

Ataxy had speed and staying power, and could run hard over 600, 700 and 750 yards – this is a rare quality. He stands alongside Mick the Miller and Brilliant Bob in his era. He really should have won the 1935 Cesarewitch, but the following year he made sure, beating Safe Rock with ease in the final. With two Classics under his collar, Ataxy had confirmed his status as one of the top dogs of 1936 and with little left to prove he was retired to stud. At stud he was not able to match his brother, Tanist, but he was the first St Leger winner and the first English Classic victor to sire a Derby champion, the 26.66 second winner of the 1940 event on his own Harringay track, G.R. Archduke.

More Cutlet?

The 1937 Cesarewitch winner was the first of the offspring of Beef Cutlet and the bitch Lady Eleanor, from the litter whelped in 1935, which also included Epinard and His Lordship. Jesmond Cutlet first hinted of his capabilities when beating Lone Keel, who was to be the Derby champion of 1938, when winning the Wood Land Stakes at the White City in May 1937. Very soon after this he entered the Scottish Derby at Carntyne, winning it with ease, making the 525 yards in 29.83 seconds, which at that point the fastest time ever for the event. He went on to take the Edinburgh Cup at Powderhall. On his return to 'the smoke' he made the Cesarewitch his own, defeating his long-time rival

Below: Grosvenor Bob

Right: Jesmond Cutlet

Grosvenor Bob in 34.56 seconds. However, come the St Leger the positions were reversed.

Throughout his career Jesmond won over £2,000. He became a powerful stud animal for a number of years. His most notable litter included two puppies from his mating with Magic Pool, Magic Beau and Magic Bohemian. Beau died young but managed to record 29.19 seconds over 525 yards at Wembley, breaking the track best as a legacy. During 1945/46 Bohemian was one of the most reliable trackers. He finished third in the 1945 Derby and won Walthamstow's Grand Prix that year. At the White City he ran the 525-yard course in 29.11 seconds to create a new national record for the distance.

Big racing

In 1937 Stanley Biss, who seemed to rule the early days of the Oaks, took West Ham dog Brave Queen to the title in a time of 29.62 seconds. The totalisator made greyhound racing phenomenally popular. By 1938 greyhound racing had more than 25 million paying customers. In that year another of Beef Cutlet's sons Ballyjoker took the West Ham Classic.

Ballyjoker was a fine racer, bred at Miss Merrett's famous Waterhall Kennels from the Future Cutlet dam, Jeanne of Waterhall. The Cesarewitch win was part of a six-month purple patch for the dog. His victories included the Wembley Summer Cup, the All England Cup at Brough Park, and the O.A. Critchley Memorial Stakes at the White City. He was the final winner of the Cesarewitch before the outbreak of the Second World War, and covered the last 600-yard

Cesarewitch course for the next eleven years in 34.02 seconds (between 1945 and 1950 West Ham's Classic was run over 550 yards).

Dogs of war

Although greyhound racing was banned at the outbreak of the Second World War, it was, after a while, allowed to continue, although it was seriously curtailed, being limited to daylight hours only. However this concession saved the lives of large numbers of dogs, although many had already been destroyed. It is a testimony to the power of track racing that it managed to continue at a time when stadium and kennel staff were being whisked off to fight, and transport to and from meetings was severely restricted. Still, it wasn't straightforward. Herbert Morrison, the Tottenham Labour MP, questioned the Home Secretary in Parliament, asking him if he was

> ... aware that women working in munitions factories for twelve hours were having to walk two or three miles to their homes because conveyances were filled with people going greyhound racing?

Photographs of full car parks at Harringay were printed in the newspapers as if the owners had committed the ultimate sin, this in spite of the fact that the 'war-dogs' involved a few tracks staging maybe a single meeting each week.

The first radio coverage of greyhound racing was from Wembley Stadium. Surprisingly, this took place as late as Easter Monday 1940, when the BBC's Raymond Glendenning broadcast the Spring Cup Final, which was won by the finest dog of the time, Junior Classic. Majestic Sandhills ran in second.

In 1940 Ken Appleton won the Laurels at Wimbledon with his West Ham-trained dog April Burglar, who was to sire a Waterloo Cup winner when retired to stud. The race was run over 500 yards when April ran to victory, covering the course 28.56 seconds from trap 3. The late Con Stevens, racing manager and then director of Wimbledon when the track opened in 1928, suggested the name of this Classic. He was the racing supremo at Wimbledon for nearly half a century. The Laurels was an original idea as most Classic greyhound races took their titles from horse racing Classics. Speedway also had its Laurels title and it is unclear if the dogs or the bikes picked up the name first, but the first Greyhound Laurels took place in 1930. As an event it is unique in the number of times it has been won by a Derby winner and for the occasions it has been won by the same dog twice – it is also notable how many home-trained animals have taken the title. In the first four decades of the event, greyhounds kenneled at Burhill were successful fifteen times.

West Ham operated daytime meetings during hostilities. In fact, there were some notable performances even at the height of the war. In 1940 Selsey Cutlet broke the 525-yard track record with a run of 29.26 seconds and in the same year Juvenile Classic ran 31.4 seconds for the 550-yard hurdles. By Beef Cutlet

Dual Grand National winner Juvenile Classic

out of Lady Eleanor, a combination of Classic breeding almost guaranteeing success, this champion hurdler was litter brother to one of the best Junior Classic. Juvenile Classic was whelped in 1936 from a second mating sire and dam. Lady Eleanor's sire was the fine hurdler Macoma, litter brother of Mick the Miller, and her dam was Nanki Poo.

Owned by Mr J.J. Cleaver, in less than three years' racing the two sons of Macoma won more than £7,000 in prize money when £100 was the sum usually awarded to a winner of a first-class event.

In his brief racing career Juvenile Classic won nearly £3,000 and seventeen trophies, which gives some indication of his class. He won the Grand National twice, in 1938 and 1940; on the latter occasion he was four years of age, his time of 30.23 was seconds faster than his first win. Only Sherry's Prince had a better record in this Classic. In three years he set up five national hurdling records over all distances, including a time of 25.88 seconds over 440 yards and 31.4 seconds when covering 550 yards. Both these times were clocked in 1938. At one point Juvenile Classic was the holder of seven hurdling records and for those three years he was unbeatable. He hardly ever stumbled when jumping. He was a dog with huge staying power and speed – qualities no doubt inherited from Beef Cutlet, his sire.

JUVENILE CLASSIC		1936 dog
Beef Cutlet	Mutton Cutlet	Jamie Miss Cinderella
	Burette	Melksham Tom Rigadoon
Lady Eleanor	Macoma	? ?
	Nanki Poo	? ?

Making a hurdler

Juvenile Classic was trained at Wembley by Joe Harmon. He died in his sleep on Christmas Day 1942, not long after his retirement. It is a shame that he was unable to pass on his racing and jumping genes.

Cook's Sandhills took the 400-yard time clocking 21.91 seconds in 1942, which was equalled the following year by the brindled dog Wireless Time, when he won the West Ham Winter Stakes. Wireless Time was one of the famous Wireless Ralley/Erin Green litter, which was so well known to greyhound followers of the time. He was one of the finest sprinters ever seen on English tracks. Whelped in April 1941, he won the West Ham September Stakes in 1942, beating Loose Lead. The following year he was victorious in the October Stakes, defeating Lizarden and the Bold Sea Rover. For a while Wireless Time held the 550-yard record as well, but his 31.24 seconds was eventually overtaken and in 1949 Drumgoon Boy's 30.53 seconds became a record that would stand forever.

Post-war boom and bust

During 1945 more than 50 million attended greyhound meetings in Britain. On average each visitor had a £5 flutter. The tote takings alone were £200 million. At the time the NGRC had licensed 77 tracks. The post-Second World War boom in greyhound racing was epitomized in the attendance at the 1946 English Derby Final, which drew a crowd of 58,000. Record wagering on the tote produced inflated profits for shareholders in the public companies that promoted the various tracks, and greyhound shares reached a new high on the stock exchange. So great were the crowds attending some tracks during the 1940s – as many as 30,000 at some meetings at West Ham, White City and

Wembley – that the gates were closed long before the first race was started. This enthusiasm did not pass unnoticed by the government, and a resultant betting tax on greyhounds (but not on horses) started a slow decline that was accelerated by the advent of television and the legalisation of betting shops.

In 1946 the American Track Operators' Association came into being with its headquarters at Miami. Its aim was to provide a common meeting ground for all track operators and for discussion to assist in track management. History suggests that it is perhaps something of a pity that British operators did not follow suit.

Kitty in a Hurry

The 1945 Cesarewitch final was actually run in 1946. Although the heats and semi-final had been run in 1945, greyhound racing was curtailed during December 1945 owing to bad weather and the shortage of fuel for electricity . The 1945 final was consequently run on 9 January 1946. The marvellous Hurry Kitty won the event.

Hurry Kitty was a fawn dog, weighing in at 55 pounds, which at that time was a fair weight for a bitch. She was whelped in April 1943. Five outstanding greyhounds contested that year's Cesarewitch. Besides the winner and runner-up, in third place was the Laurels winner Burhill Moon and in fourth spot Kilcora Master. The Oakes winner Prancing Kitty came home fifth. The quality of the field is a testament to Kitty's power and stamina. She was the first bitch to take the title.

Hurry Kitty's dam's sire was none other than the Cesarewitch winner of a decade earlier, the noble Brilliant Bob. Hurry Kitty's nine-and-a-half length final winning margin from Gala Flash was the biggest in the history of the race or of any other Classic. She had won her first-round heat by twelve lengths from Jonwell Shamrock and her semi-final by six lengths. She was one of a group of superb long-distance runners about in the forties sired by Castledown Lad (others included Coyne's Castle and Shaggy Lass). Her dam was Brilliant Gay,

The White Housing

Home sweet home

who was amongst the exceptional bitches sired by Brilliant Bob. Brilliant Gay had run up for the 1941 Irish Coursing Oaks, and was victorious in the Leinster Puppy Stakes at Enniscorthy. As such she demonstrated herself to be an exceptional animal on the coursing field and track.

As her dam had done before her, Hurry Kitty won the Leinster Puppy Stakes in the same time as Brilliant Gay, 30.5 seconds. At Shelbourne Park in the Easter Cup she came in a creditable third in 29.86, behind Astra. Following this encounter she was bought by Miss Kitty Kwasnik at a price of £2,000, at that point the biggest sum ever paid for a bitch, although not long after that another Castledown Lad bitch, Castledown Tiptoes, was bought for £3,000, the highest fee laid out for a bitch in Ireland.

Not long after arriving in Britain Hurry Kitty, with a time of 17.17 seconds, set a new record for 300 yards at Monmor Green in Wolverhampton. It was at this venue that she won the second October Stakes, beating the equally valuable Gala Flash by five lengths. However, it was in the Cesarewitch at West Ham, over 550 yards, that she was to reach her peak. She won her heat by twelve lengths, humbling Jonwell Shamrock. The semi-final saw her defeat Kilcora Master by six lengths. The final ran to form and she beat Gala Flash in 31.26 seconds and nearly ten lengths. This was to stand as the biggest margin of victory in the Cesarewitch at West Ham.

After a brief rest, Hurry Kitty turned up at Wembley to contest the first Trial Stakes. She had lost none of her form. She won her heat in front of Fair and Handsome and then took the final from Overtime in 30.16 seconds. This was her thirteenth race in Britain and she had won eleven of them. This record was achieved over all distances, proving her to be an almost unbeatable animal. Miss Kwasnik issued a challenge of £5,000 for a match to be staged anywhere in the country between her bitch and any other, but then Hurry Kitty went in to season and the challenge was never met. She had a few more races, but her competitive career was as good as over.

Hurry Kitty was one of the marvellous three she-dogs of the mid-1940s that also included Shaggy Lass and Robeen Printer. This trio were three of the best bitches ever to race in England.

Colonel Skookrum won the 'real' 1946 and the second Cesarewitch final of that year in a time of 31.28 seconds. The first year of peace following the Second World War saw the first greyhound appear on television. Trev's Perfection was shown with his owner-trainer Fred Trevillion and several of his other dogs.

Lilac whine

Lilac's Luck recorded the fasted ever time over 700 yards at West Ham in 1946, his 39.88 seconds was to be the last word at that distance, at least as far as the East End's track was concerned. A blue brindle son of Printer out of Wilton Sandhills, Lilac was whelped in December 1943. He was to become one of the finest middle-distance dogs and a member of the very exclusive group of animals to reach the finals of both the Irish and English Derbys.

Lilac's Luck was bought for just £400 at the Shelbourne Park sales by Major A.E. Allnatt; and not long after, in 1945, he won the Irish Derby, defeating Gun Music by two lengths in a time of 30.23 seconds. He was the first champion to have avoided defeat throughout the event. Later in the year he won the Trigo Cup, which was to become the Guinness Ulster Derby, in 29.65 seconds, an extremely swift run. Thirty years on, Piping Rock's time was something less than a length's improvement.

In that 1945 event Lilac's Luck beat Mad Tanist and Astra, then thought to be Ireland's speediest animals. He also competed well in the National Sprint before arriving in Britain at the start of 1946. He had come to take a tilt at the Derby and try to become the first dog to do the Irish/English Derby double. Kennelled at Dorchester, where he was placed with trainer R. Jones, in his first race at Reading he set a new record for the 550 yards, clocking 31.42 seconds. At Wembley he won his heat for the Gold Cup beating Shaggy Lass by five lengths, demonstrating his devastating speed. He went on to win the final by five lengths, humiliating Western Dasher in 40.06 seconds.

Lilac's Luck in action

Now joint favourite for the Derby, he fought his way to the final to face Monday's News. This great dog was at the height of his powers. Lilac's Luck, although running a spirited race, was beaten into runner-up position by a new final record run of 29.34 seconds, but he put the likes of Plucky Hero, Celtic Chief, Dante II and Shannon Shore behind him (in that order).

During 1946, alongside Monday's News, Lilac was the best dog in training. At Hull in April he set a new track record for the 700 yards, defeating Alvaston Lulu Belle by two-and-a-half lengths in 41.32 seconds. At Shawfield he ran up to Mad Midnight when that hound broke the track and world record over 700 yards with a time of 39.55 seconds. It was not long after this that he claimed his West Ham speed record winning the Second July Stakes, from there he was flown to Ireland to take part in the National Sprint Championships at Dunmore Park, contesting the 435 yards he again made the final. However, he was withdrawn from the race with an injured foot. The event was to be won by Count Lally.

At this point Lilac was sent to stud having proved himself one of the great dogs of racing history.

Even more taxing

In the 1947 Budget a 10 per cent tax was imposed on all greyhound betting, causing the tote to pay out considerably less to the backer. At the same time there was also less money for the tracks to retain to pay overheads, as the 10 per cent tax was deductible before the tracks were allowed to deduct their own 6 per cent. The ruling came into force on 1 January 1948, a time when petrol rationing was ending, enabling people to spend more time in their cars. During the same period television was starting up and this attracted many former punters away from the sport. The fuel crisis caused all tracks to close for six weeks from 1947 to 1948 and limited racing until 1949. This convergence of short-sighted financial decisions and global economic conditions again effectively cut greyhound racing attendance, and exacerbated the spiral of decline.

Two more wonderful bitches contested the 1947 Cesarewitch – Rio Cepretta and Izadaisy. Both reached the final, which was an exciting affair. It was uncertain all the way; right up to the finishing line at least three dogs were in with a chance. Red Tan and Izdaisy crossed as one. But it was Red Tan who took the title by a neck, with Parish Model in third place, half a length behind. Red Tan ran the Cesarewitch 550-yard course in 31.3 seconds.

A three Classic hound

1948 was the year that Local Interprize won the three Classics, including the Cesarewitch – in this race he beat Freckled Major by just under two lengths in 30.88 seconds, the first time 31 seconds had been beaten over the 550-yard version of the Classic.

Local Interprize

Local Interpize was a black dog by Ruby Boarder out of Mystical Daisy. His grand sire was the renowned Creamery Border, from whom he probably inherited his phenomenal speed out of the traps and his keen intellect. He belonged to Mr Eric W. Goddard, a butcher from Sheffield and was trained at Clapton by the former West Ham trainer Stanley Biss. From 1948 to 1949 Interprize won in excess of £6,000 and many have argued that he was amongthe best dogs ever to run in Britain up to his era.

The first British race for Local Interprize came at Powder Hall in Edinburgh at the end of 1947; this is when he faced the famous bitch Sheevaun in the Scottish Puppy Derby. This was the start of a two-year run of success, replicating the 1946/47 achievements of Monday's News, an animal gifted with the same kind of intelligence and swiftness from the traps. When Monday's News left competitive racing, Local Interprize filled the vacuum. He attracted huge crowds at the top London tracks; sometimes over 50,000 people would turn out to watch him perform. Monday's News and Local Interprize had been in the right places at the right time, when the popularity of greyhound racing was at its height. They in turn were followed by Priceless Border and Endless

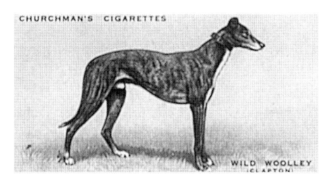

Wild Woolley

Gossip in the lineage of all-time great dogs.

Like Mick the Miller, Wild Woolley, Monday's News and later on Dante II, Local Interprize was a slim and solid creature. He was an efficient runner, never running out at bends and quick to take advantage of any hint of an opportunity to grab the rails and hold on to them. He didn't do much to catch the eye during the first months of 1948, so when he turned up at Catford in May for the Gold Collar, his first Classic, there were few punters who bothered to give him a second look. However, he made the crowd sit up and stare when he won his heat by three lengths, murdering Royal Canopy, the favourite. As the traps for the semi-final flew open, it was Local Interprize who hit the track as favourite. He didn't disappoint, defeating Tell Nobody by a blinding eight lengths. The final came and went without giving him a problem. He claimed the £600 purse by a yard from Kerry Rally. The quarter-mile circuit suited Local Interprize and provided an impressive stage for his London debut.

In June our hero trotted out onto the huge White City track to compete in the English Derby. In his heat he had to deal with Mazurka, but he moved on to finish second to Priceless Border in his semi-final. The fine brindle that belonged to Mr O'Kane was to beat him again in the final by two lengths, but Priceless had to run a record time of 28.78 seconds to do so. So July arrived and Local Interprize was out on his home track of Clapton for the Scurry Gold Cup over the quarter-mile. Stanley Biss was of the opinion that shorter distances were right for him, but Local Interprize was defeated in both his heat and semi-final by Ironmonger, the animal that would start the final as favourite to win the title. But come the last round it was Local Interprize who made the front first and he went on to win the race by an inordinate eight lengths from Clonroche Lad, crossing the line in 23.04 seconds. It was the largest winning margin in the entire history of the Scurry Cup and the fastest time in its two-decade history.

Four days later, Local Interprize was in the traps at Cardiff awaiting the start of the Welsh Derby. He won both his heat and the final by seven lengths from West End Dasher in 29.32 seconds, taking the record for the event and at the same time creating a new track record. The Welsh Derby wasn't a Classic then, but it was to be given that status some years later. As such, Local Interprize could arguably boast that in his first three months of racing that season he had been victorious in three Classics and had run up for the Derby. At the time this was an unequalled record.

Before the end of the year Stanley Biss had the inspiration to test Local Interprize over a longer distance. His Cesarewitch win proved his stamina and he hushed those who had whispered doubts by winning his fourth Classic in a year. Such an accomplishment was without parallel in Britain and Ireland. However, the Pall Mall still awaited his presence in December. Winning his heat and the semi-final, he was made 2-1 for the final. He looked good from the traps but ended up in third place. However, 1948 had seen him bring home more than £4,000 in winnings, helping Biss to a total of £20,000 in prizes, an amount never before reached by a trainer.

Local Interprize took a break after all this success and he wasn't seen until the spring of 1949, when at Stamford Bridge, on May 14, he beat Ballymac Ball by almost two lengths; this greyhound was making its debut in Britain, but he was to be the Derby winner the following year. Seven days on Local Interprize attempted to retain his Gold Collar at Catford. He finished an unpromising third in his heat and was beaten by almost a length in his semi-final by Killure Lad, a 20-1 outsider. His followers thus had every right to be nervous as the dogs were paraded for the final. A return to his best meant that Local Interprize romped home by four and a half lengths, leaving Laughing Grenadier looking very glum in the wake of his 25.88 second run. This made him the first and only dog ever to win the event on two occasions. He now laid claim to a fistful of Classics, an achievement unsurpassed by any other greyhound on British soil.

June saw Interprize make the Derby final at White City yet again. The England born and bred bitch Narrogar Ann was too much for him, as was Dangerous Prince one-and-a-half lengths behind her. Local Interprize could do no better than fourth. A month went by and once more he faced the challenge of the Scurry Cup which, like the Gold Collar, is a sprinter's Classic. Of course he had two Gold Collars and one Scurry Cup to his name, so a win would make him one of the immortals as no dog had won two Scurry Cups, let alone two Scurry Cups and two Gold Collars.

The atmosphere was electric even in the heats of 9 July, however it was not until 14 July that his first race, heat six, was run. He faced the Irish hound Burndennet Brook, a 6-1 on favourite. Both greyhounds left the traps like banshees, but Local Interprize was in no mood to take second place and came home three-and-a-half lengths to the good, covering the course in 23.13 seconds, the fastest of the eight heats by a long way. The two swiftest animals were in different heats of the second round. Burndennet Brook came home in third place and was fortunate to qualify for the semi-final. Local Interprize beat Magna Leader in the quickest time of the heats that far. The semi-finals found these explosive dogs in different races; both won – Local Interprize by a staggering ten lengths in 22.99 seconds, the first time 23 seconds had been broken in the Classic.

This set up a really juicy final on 23 July. Clapton Stadium crammed in 30,000 punters. Could Local Interprize do the impossible? He paraded as 6-4 on favourite. As they were liberated from their starting cages the two fliers cannoned to the front accompanied by a massive roar from the crowd. Burndennet Brook had the favoured trap 1 whilst Interprize came out of trap 6. The first turn's sway saw Burndennet in front, but Interprize was fighting. Welded together the two hounds rounded the final bend, not a chink of light between them – they flashed across the line as a single entity. The murmur went out that the race was a dead heat. Crowd, trainers, owners and dogs waited and waited for the lights to speak on the tote board, then the simple message came ... first no.1; second no.6. Burndennet had won by the shortest of short heads.

Local Interprize went looking for a second Cesarewitch win, but in his heat he came up against Sailing at Dawn. The latter hit his best form and set a new track record of 30.77 seconds. Local Interprize stopped there, seemingly discouraged. Along with Ballymac Ball he was at Harringay for the Pall Mall, but they both failed to find a place in the final. Past his best he had been set up at 33-1, the rank outsider. It was a sad sight for many of his loyal supporters, most of whom thought his racing career should have been terminated at its height, but he had shown himself to be the finest sprinter in the annals of greyhound racing. His Pall Mall run of 25 November 1949 was his curtain call.

Eric Goddard did not try to purchase another greyhound – in two years he had seen his dog do wonders. For his few hundred pounds he had ridden a dream that could not possibly have been emulated.

The last Cesarewitch of the 1940s was won by the fawn dog Drumgoon Boy. In his heat he beat the Derby winner Narrogar Ann by six lengths in 30.54 seconds. Seemingly unsatisfied 'The Boy' bettered this by 0.01 seconds when winning his semi-final. In the final he equalled his own track record.

> April Burglar has won the Laurels,
> So there can be no more quarrels,
> That Ken Appleton is a trainer of note,
> Even when his dog wears a white coat,
> For Wimbledon's proud trophy was nicked,
> By the dog West Ham punters picked,
> He galloped home like a getaway car,
> And was the best greyhound by far,
> Now he's a shining Classic star,
> Our springtime robber, April Burglar.
>
> From 'The Ballad of the West Ham Dogs'

7
THE GLORIOUS BEGINNING OF THE INEVITABLE END

The stadium awaits

Many tracks were opened in the provinces as well as in Ireland, and in June of 1927 the Stadium at The White City in London threw open its doors. Here again the experience of Manchester was repeated, the proceedings on the first night being witnessed by a crowd of 25,000, which was surpassed on the second night by at least another 5,000, and in a few as many as 70,000 were present. Soon after the track at Harringay was opened, thus converting waste ground to a remunerative purpose.

Croxton Smith, A. (1927) *Greyhound Racing and Breeding.*
Gay and Hancock Ltd, London

Looking back at West Ham greyhound racing and its context does not really fit the nature of the sport and by association those involved in it. If you have any contact with the track, or more particularly if you make a relationship with greyhound racing later in life, you will be struck by the existential attitude it seems to nurture. As one enters greyhound racing as a culture, one becomes bound up with the moment; life is set in the present and the future is curtailed to the horizons by the next race, with the occasional leap forward to the coming Derby, Cesarewitch or National. To that extent it is an escape from reality, but it sets up an encounter with an alternative actuality. Expectations are a restless mixture of boundless optimism and cynical propriety, often vacillating violently from pole to pole. The past takes on the shape of an archive of form or extraordinary departures from the same, its only relevance being to interpret the current situation – today's racecard.

When I went to West Ham dogs this tightly encompassed veracity seemed to be embodied in the pages of *The Greyhound Life* or *The Greyhound Magazine*. The minutiae of a greyhound's life accrue and enter the warp and weft of existence via the repetition of the track and its functioning. The parade of dogs, expectation building to the loading into the traps, the solemnity that reigns over the seconds between the stand lights fading and the off; the race itself, a charge, cosseted within the exuberance of the crowd; the result. Then it all starts again. The present is preserved by the process of the meeting and the progression of meetings that seem to promise a kind of eternity in their predictable reoccurrence. The chaos and panic of the race are caught within the circular march of events of which West Ham and its Cesarewitch were a part. Time is frozen by this collusion of event and persona.

Even the architecture of some tracks epitomise and emphasize this abandonment of time in the ordinary sense. West Ham Stadium was like a Wild West town; it had a pioneer feel to it. It was Dodge City, complete with its Jessie James. It was Tombstone, featuring Wyatt Earp, Judge Wells Spicer, Doc Holliday and Big Nose Kate, the Clantons and the McLaurys. It had a Boot Hill, a saloon, and an OK corral. It had gunslingers, sheriffs, marshals and judges. Set in the 'badlands' of the docks that were in the process of shrinkage for much of its history, the stadium's wide open spaces were held together by crumbling architecture that was once solid and grand, for a short while, but had been transformed into 'Make-do-and-mendville'. It seemed to be held together by six-inch nails. It was almost darned in places by recycled timber and corrugated iron. You could sometimes trace where these materials had been requisitioned from: Fifes Bananas, HMS *Penn*, The Colorado Oil Inc., and the one that most fascinated me as a boy, Thomas Mann, Cobbler to the King, Damascus. This was the dam of detritus that held the future at bay. More contemporaneously one can understand the turrets and lines of Walthamstow Greyhound Track carrying out the same function. This is a fortress that defends its interior from the effects of history and the wider context. Its artistic influences are those that straddled the period between the wars. Egocentric, ecstatic, eccentric, the whole structure sweeps one into a space that could be any moment between 1925 and now. It is telling that its façade is reminiscent of a castle or, with the iron-bars of its car park, a prison. But it is a stately fortress, perhaps built to hold some great and beautiful Empress. She, maybe, is the Queen of Time.

Loves and lovers

The dogs offer a life within a life, a parallel existence. All supporters of sport inhabit this dodecahedron of loving innocence. Such love is all of a piece. The punter who makes up the backbone of greyhound racing does not love just one dog, although one dog might exemplify all that is beautiful in the sport. As a supporter of the track I need the successes, but also the failures it confronts me with. This is what makes it real and frames its elements of fantasy. My football

RACING EVERY

MONDAY AND WEDNESDAY

at 8 p.m.

Throughout October the Wednesday Meetings at West Ham will be the only Greyhound Race Meetings in the Metropolitan area.

At each meeting the pick of the World's best greyhounds will be competing in Open and Restricted events, and every race will be worth coming to see.

£1,000 GREYHOUND CESAREWITCH.

This last Classic race of the year will commence on October 28th.

The Win-Place and Forecast Totalisators cater for every individual taste.

East End dreams.

team, West Ham United, do something of the same thing for me. They are not Arsenal or Manchester United. They fail, at times abysmally. But every now and then they will soar to giddying heights, producing art and beauty, and the awful dreaded panoply of mediocrity out of which this erupts makes that single turn, that one sublime pass, that wonderful goal, all the more stupendous. No inhabitant of the Stadium of Dreams will know this, for they live in a constant dream. If this is broken they will up-sticks and be off to the next venue that can, apparently, protect them from the painful growth offered in failure and debacle, to Arsenal, Liverpool, Chelsea or some other depot of alacrity for false paradise.

Greyhound racing will not allow such options. It offers fulfillment but is guaranteed to frustrate. That is its allure, its grace is that it can be a 'fucker', a gorgeous, tantalizing 'mare' of a thing. It leaves its lover wanting more but resenting what it has taken. Aficionados will be subject to demands. This is no massage parlour of a sport. Suitors and admirers will have to do something. You will be drawn back, needing to understand it, beat it, win. You think it might love you because you love it and you go back again and again to explore this potential. It is love because it offers a pain that you don't want to lose. It hurts so much and it would be such a relief if it stopped, but if it stopped you might forget you are alive, because the pain confirms that you are living and that's what you really, really love.

As such, the stories of dogs, their tales, can never capture what they are or the affinity anyone has to the sport they inhabit. But these histories are the narrative nets that engulf the dogs and the appeal of the sport. The West Ham track gave a home to their exploits and a stage on which the myths and legends that sustain 'the dogs' could be wrought. It is for the reader to create that magic, energize the mythology from the materiality of these animals, as the mighty West Ham crowd once did as it watched, punted, cheered and cried, creating a world outside of time.

The final bend

The 1952 Cesarewitch was won in 33.24 seconds by Magourna Reject. By Astra's Son out of Saucy Dame, he was thought by some greyhound experts to be one of the top ten dogs in the sport's history. He was a good-looking brindle who inherited the speed and staying power of his grand dam Astra, who was mated with Castledown Lad sire Paddy the Champion to produce Astra's Son, also a terrific sire.

Magourna Reject was bought by Mrs Frances Chandler who placed the animal with the Walthamstow trainer Mrs Frances Chandler. He was to emulate Ballymac Ball and Endless Gossip in terms of pulling and exciting spectators. He was one of a string of greyhounds to grace the 1950s, the golden era of the tracks; these included Duet Leader, Ford Spartan, Pigalle Wonder and Mile Bush Pride. However, Magourna Pride was the best over the longer distances, his victory time of 39.88 seconds in the 1953 Wembley St Leger over 700 yards was

The number board

beaten only by Dante II, in the first quarter century of the race. That was the first televised event. He ran wonderfully in that year's Cesarewitch, recording the fastest time for the 600-yard version of the event to that date. Tommy Reilly was to take over as his trainer before Magourna Reject took the Coronation Cup at Monmore Green. He went on to win the Steward's Cup at Gloucester, defeating Dashing Ash and Galtee Cleo by two lengths, setting a new track record in doing so.

Magourna Reject was the sire of Chittering Hope, dam of the 1965 Derby winner Chittering Clapton from a mating with Noted Crusader, but failed to sire any other top performing dog.

MAGOURNA REJECT		March 1950 blue & brindled dog
Astra's Son	Paddy The Champion	Castletown Lad Brilliant Gay
	Astra	Tanist Mad Darkie
Saucy Dame	Ballymakeera Gift	Ammon Carb Old Capwell
	Another Dame	Tiro Dame Of The House

In 1955 Gulf of Darien became the first Cesarewitch winner to break 33 seconds. Three years later came the wonderful final that ended in a dead heat between the brindle Pigalle Wonder and Rylane Pleasure, the only occasion that a Classic race in Britain had concluded in such a manner.

Pigalle Wonder was by Champion Prince out of the famous dam Prairie Champion. He challenged Future Cutlet and Endless Gossip in his looks;

having a lustrous coat and attractive lines he appeared a total champion. In common with other top sporting greyhounds he would have been hard to beat on the show bench if he had not been involved in racing. He was whelped in March 1956 and made his competitive debut on 10 October 1957 at Kilkenny in a heat of the McCalmont Cup. He took the race by ten lengths in a time of 29.8 seconds, going on to win the final, illustrating what a fine animal he was at the tender age of one and a half years. He was purchased by Mr Al Burnett, the owner of the London based Pigalle Club, following a 29.1 second 525-yard trial at Harold's Cross and he was renamed Pigalle Wonder. He lived up to his new name over his three-year career. He won nearly £8,000 at a time when £1,500 was the prize for victory in the Derby. However he probably earned more than that at stud.

When Pigalle ran his incredible speed, together with his intelligence, drew large crowds. He had a people-pulling power not seen since Mick the Miller and Monday's News. He was able to get out of the traps like a bullet from a gun and never knew what it was to give up, taking on all conditions and tracks (he set track records on the seven most prestigious venues in Britain). His 28.44 second win in the Derby semi-final stood as a record for the event for a decade until Yellow Printer ran 28.3 seconds in 1968. But he had barely got through his first-round heat, having been given third place by a nose, a margin of something like an inch.

Pigalle Wonder went on to be placed at Wembley with Jim Snyder junior and in 1958 found himself 5-4 on in the English Derby final. His odds were about right. He won by three lengths in 28.65 seconds, beating Northern Lad and Mile Bush Pride, the winner in 1959. Pigalle was just two lengths slower than Endless Gossip's hand time of 28.5 seconds. His next challenge came at Harringay in the Pall Mall. He ran to victory with consummate ease, covering the 525 yards in 29.03 seconds. This time was not bettered during the period that the event was run over this distance until Local Motive made 28.86 seconds ten years later (this stood until 1975, when the distance was altered to metres).

Pigalle Wonder had demonstrated his class as a middle-distance runner, but he finished an outstanding year dead-heating with Ryane Pleasure in the Cesarewitch final. He had set new standards on every track he ran on that year. At Wembley over 525 yards his 28.78-second run on 26 May 1958 was unmatched up to the time the race was converted to metres – over twenty years.

On 13 August 1960 Pigalle Wonder ran in his final contest. It took place at Shelbourne Park, the final of the Irish Derby. He had run up to Perry's Apple in his semi-final and was beaten by the same animal and The Black Ranger in the final following problems on the first bend. However, Pigalle was then four-and-a-half years old. He moved on to start a decade-long career as a stud dog. In the first part of 1963 Mr Burnett sold his dog to Mr A.S. Lucas of Bray, County Wicklow, to stand stud in Ireland. He went for the staggering sum of £3,500, the biggest fee ever laid out for a greyhound finished with racing. But the dog surely paid back his owner many times over. Like Brilliant Bob two decades

OGDEN'S CIGARETTES

STANLEY TRACK, LIVERPOOL. 2.

Stanley Park. The West Ham of the North

earlier, he became the famous sire of many fine bitches; having a number of outstanding dams in his lineage he passed on their qualities as well as his own speed and trackcraft. Alongside Macoma and Brilliant Bob and his contemporary The Grand Fire he was able to leave his mark through the female line. A dam with his blood achieved great value, with Irish breeders in particular.

However, one of Pigalle Wonder's finest progeny was one of his first, and a dog. He was to replicate his sire's capabilities as a racer and transmit the same to his offspring. Wonder Valley, a winner of the Irish Derby, also left his mark on the world of coursing. Kyle Guest and Ballyard Jumbo, winner and runner-up respectively of the Irish Coursing Derby at Clonmel in 1979, were of his line, as was the Coursing Oaks winner Little Treasure.

Mated to Shandaroba, Pigalle Wonder produced the wonderful Russian Gun, who won the 1968 Irish Derby. He also ran up to Yellow Printer in the final of 1969. Russian Gun was sire of An Tain, dam of Tain Mor, who was victorious in the Irish Derby in 1976; this dog sired Desert Pilot. Russian Gun, mated to Sheila's Prize, gave Pampered Peggy, dam of Pampered Rover. Russian Gun appears in the bottom quarter, as the maternal great grand-sire of Whisper Wishes' pedigree. He was the winner of the final Derby at White City in 1984. This maintained Pigalle Wonder's connection with the stadium wherein he performed so well.

From his mating with The Grand Fire bitch Survival, Pigalle Wonder sired Martin's Pigalle, dam of Highland Finch, who was dam of Lacca Champion, the winner of the English Derby in 1978 and runner-up the following year. A younger sister of Martin's Pigalle, More Wonder was dam of Kilmagoura Fair, who was dam of the 1978 Oaks and 1979 St Leger victor Kilmagoura Mist. From a mating with Rather Fancy, Pigalle Wonder sired Yurituni, who was dam of the litter brothers Cobbler and Sole Aim, the 1971 Irish Derby Champion. This greyhound sired Columbcille Aim, dam of the speedy bitch Penny County, who took the Irish Derby in 1979. Cobbler, and thus Yurituni, appear in the dam line of triple Scurry Gold Cup champion Yankee Express, who was by the American sire Pecos Jerry. Mated to Red Cavier, Pigalle Wonder sired Paradise Wonder, dam of Paradise Spectre, who won the Classic Grand Prix at Walthamstow on two occasions. With Narod Queen Pigalle Wonder sired Sabrina, dam to Instant Gambler, the Welsh Derby winner.

A later son was Fantastic Prize, sire of the Irish Derby champion of 1972 Catsrock Daisy – this was amongst the swiftest of bitches ever. Pigalle Wonder was also the sire of Shady Begonia, who reached the 1968 English Derby final and the Cesarewitch of the same year. It won the Midlands St Leger and the Sportsview Trophy of 1968. He ran his last race at Owlerton, winning for the fifty-eighth time in a two-year career.

In the history of greyhound sport Pigalle Wonder is only rivalled by Brilliant Bob in terms of his contribution as a racer and sire. Sole Aim and Russian Gun might also be mentioned in the same breath but they are both from Pigalle Wonder. He died aged nearly thirteen year early in January 1969. He made a powerful impact on racing in the latter part of the twentieth century.

PIGALLE WONDER		March 1956 brindled dog
Champion Prince	Bella's Prince	Castletown Lad Bella's Witch
	Sallywell	Swanky Jog Lucy Lilla
Prairie Peg	The Grand Champion	Mad Tanist Could Be Worse
	Prairie Vixen	Astra's Son Take Murex

The fifties flew

In 1958 the BBC inaugurated their famous TV Sportsview Trophy. From 1961 to 1975 it was run over 880 yards, with a first prize of £1,750 at a different venue each year. The first time it was run over 500 yards at Wimbledon and won by Town Prince in 28.14 seconds. The following year the cameras came to West Ham for the first and last time and Don't Divulge took the honours over 700 yards in 38.72 seconds. Trainer L. Reynolds had been responsible for both these Trophy winners.

The last Cesarewitch said goodbye to the 1950s with the victory of Mile Bush Pride. By Grand Champion out of Witching Dancer, MBP was whelped in 1956. This brindle was bred by Mrs Nora Johnson of Campile, County Wexford and was reared by Mrs Hannah Malone. He was to have quite an impact on the racing world, being a consistent racer with a good turn of speed. But perhaps more importantly, Mile Bush Pride was a courageous dog with good track

RACING EVERY

MONDAY AND WEDNESDAY

at 8 p.m.

Throughout October the Wednesday Meetings at West Ham will be the only Greyhound Race Meetings in the Metropolitan area.

TO-MORROW

Open Sudden Death Sweepstakes

— 400 yards Flat —

£1,000 GREYHOUND CESAREWITCH.

This last Classic race of the year will commence on October 28th.

The Win-Place and Forecast Totalisators cater for every individual taste.

Everyone a winner

sense. This collection of fine qualities made him arguably one of the top three dogs of the 1950s, alongside Ford Spartan and Pigalle Wonder.

After repeated attempts to win the Greyhound Derby, having put thousands of pounds into the project through the purchase of top animals, Noel Purvis, a ship owner and greyhound enthusiast, bought Mile Bush Pride at the start of 1958. He placed the dog with Jack Harvey at Wembley specifically to prepare the greyhound for that year's Premier event. MBP was not yet two years of age when he reached the final of the Derby; if he had taken the title he would have been the youngest ever winner, but he found Pigalle Wonder, coming out of trap 1, just too much. 'The Wonder' won for Al Burnett, in a photo-timing record for the event (this was the first time this had been used for the Derby). Mile Bush Pride had been beaten by a neck for the runner-up place.

Over the next year owner and trainer rationed Mile Bush Pride's racing, keeping his competitive appearances to a minimum, all the time focusing on the 1959 Derby. MBP went through to the final undefeated and into the last stage as even money favourite. He won what was one of the most exciting Derby finals ever by the narrowest of margins. Three dogs crossed the line as one; the subsequent photo revealed that Mile Bush Pride had beaten Snub Nose by a neck. Crazy Parachute was as a short head behind.

About a week later, Mile Bush Pride went to Carntyne and won the Scottish Derby in 29.41 seconds. Next stop was Cardiff Arms Park for the Welsh Derby which he also made his own, breaking the track record with a 28-second run that was never to be beaten. This grand slam equalled the earlier achievements of Trev's Perfection. The Cesarewitch completed a phenomenal year for Mile Bush Pride. His 32.66 seconds was to stand as the fastest time for the event whilst it was held at West Ham.

At almost four years of age MBP was entered for the 1960 Derby, but he reached the final for the third successive year, starting as 5-4 on favourite. Crowded on the first turn and obliged to check, he let Duleek Dandy take the rails and the outsider won by two lengths from Clonalvy Romance, who was a length in front of Mile Bush Pride. Purvis had seen enough and retired his champion.

The sixties squeeze

In 1960 the Greyhound Derby at White City was televised by the BBC and it became a regular feature of its sports programming for many years. The winner of that first televised race and its £2,000 prize was Duleek Dandy. At 25-1 the dog was the biggest outsider to win the event.

As the 1950s gave way to the 1960s, attendance at greyhound meetings was still in decline. The 1960 amendment to the Betting and Lotteries Act of 1934 meant that the tax on on-course betting was fixed at five per cent, whilst off-course wagers were subject to six per cent deductions. Though this was of some benefit to the tracks, the difference between the on-course and off-

The track... the challenge

course tax of only one per cent was not sufficient to bring back those who had deserted greyhound racing. Other entertainment and gambling options, such as bingo and football pools, offered considerably more prize money for a small outlay. The 1961 legalisation that enabled betting shops to operate in the high street was another huge blow to the tracks.

At the start of the 1960s, television began to rule leisure time. There was also a greater variety of outdoor entertainment than had been on offer in the immediate post-Second World War period. Attendance at greyhound tracks had fallen to 14 million from 5,736 meetings in 1960 and the tote turnover was £54 million. By 1967, although tote turnover from 6,000 meetings had risen to £66 million, attendance was down to 10 million. At the end of the 'swinging' decade, the future of the sport was clouded by the mounting pressures of takeover bids from property developers as the land value of greyhound tracks appreciated.

Attendance at Greyhound Meetings in Britain 1927-71

Year	Total
1927	5,656,686
1928	13,695,275
1929	15,855,162
1930	17,119,120
1931	17,906,917
1932	20,178,260
1939	26,000,000
1945	
(109 tracks)	50,000,000
1960	14,243,808
1967	10,000,000
1971	7,119,398

In the USA, except New York State, there was no legalized off-course betting, and as such attendance at tracks had increased every year since 1920. At the start of the last quarter of the twentieth century, tote takings in America amounted to more than $100 million annually. The seven states that permitted greyhound racing collected more than $70 million each year in tax, the state of Florida contributing about half of this amount. As West Ham was closing, track attendance in the USA had been rising by about eight per cent annually for the previous decade and was to continue to grow over the coming years. A 20,000 attendance at a meeting was not uncommon; the sport and all connected with it were earning more than $1 billion annually. Massachusetts, Arizona and Arkansas are the most important States. Looking at the comparative situation, one can't help but think in terms of golden eggs and the needless slaughter of generous geese. In Britain in 1945 there were seventy-seven tracks; now there are less than forty. In 1946 there was a crowd of 50,000 cheering on the English Derby winner Monday's News; when Lartigue Note won the same event in 1989, fewer than 10,000 bothered to turn up.

The punter's revenge

In all this the proverbial buck stopped at the punters. Tax and costs – material, financial, emotional and spiritual – were passed on to them. However, the British greyhound fan has always been more than a spectator, and often quite prepared and able to strike back. In Britain, off-course betting operates on starting price returns from the track. In the 1960s, in order to increase track attendance, promoters refused to allow infringement of their tote dividend copyright. This change also had the effect of preventing a certain type of betting coup – rigging the tote. This was done by investing large amounts on the tote on outsiders at tracks with weak attendance figures, in order to extend the price of the favourite, which could be heavily backed in betting shops.

The Classic case of such a coup occurred in the 'far east end', Dagenham, in Essex, not too far from West Ham greyhound stadium, in 1964. A brilliant plan involving a team of 90 people queuing at 31 tote windows produced the amazing result of just one winning forecast ticket worth £987 11s 9d, representing odds of nearly 9,875-1. Delaying tactics by the team kept the tote windows clear of other punters while money was poured on combinations involving rank outsiders. One ticket only was purchased on each of the favourite combinations, and the result went according to plan. Meanwhile collaborators were placing bets on the favourite combinations at betting shops around the country. It was never discovered how much was laid, but every £100 invested off the course on the winning combination would win nearly a million pounds.

In the event, the bookmakers refused to pay up, and it was only after several court cases that the Dagenham track paid out on the winning ticket two years later.

The Monalee Era

Tommy Johnston was the outstanding trainer at West Ham in the early 1960s. He won the Pall Mall in 1962 with Hurry the King and the following year he nursed Music Guest to Gold Collar victory. It was the first time that event had been raced over 570 yards and Music Guest clocked 33.36 seconds for the distance out of trap 5. Apart from its second running in 1934, the Gold Collar had previously used a 440-yard course. Always run at Catford, it was a prestigious event offering £5,000 to the winner in 1979 and £10,000 in 1990.

An extraordinary dog turned up at the Cesarewitch in 1966. It was Monalee Champion's NGRC debut. He won his first heat in 33.11 seconds the fastest of the round for the 600 yards. He went on to win his second-round heat but finished down the field in his semi-final, and although he went into the consolation as 5-4 favourite he finished fifth. The final was eventually won by the biggest-priced Classic winner of all time, the 66-1 chance Rostown Victor, who clocked 34.06 seconds. But the young black dog was destined for a much brighter future than that year's winner. Whelped in September 1964, Monalee was to become arguably the most successful track sire of the second part of the twentieth century. Tipping the scales at 67lb, he arrived in Britain three months after Geoff Hurst's World Cup hat-trick. He had reached the final of Enniscorthy's April Stakes and the semi-finals of the Irish Derby but was proving a real problem for trainer Ger McKenna as he was being a bad grubber. McKenna suggested the dog would do better in a small kennel and a deal was reached with Watford greengrocer Don Price. Monalee had already been entered in the Hackney Sales and although he never actually appeared at the track, the sales regulations insisted that he be offered for sale. He made 610 guineas and joined the Hemel Hempstead kennel of private trainer Frank Conlon.

After the Cesarewitch, Monalee went on the open race circuit and won over 525 yards at Harringay in 29.41 seconds. Behind him was Laurels winner Super Fame. He then appeared at Stamford Bridge and won a 700-yard open by nine lengths in 39.39 seconds. He returned to four bends and won a £400, 550-yard open at White City by seven and half lengths in 30.14 seconds as the 4-9 favourite.

Monalee Champion completed a four-timer when winning the fastest heat of the Cobb 700 in 39.66 seconds, being the hot 1-3 favourite. Once again he lost out in the final, going down to Trojan Silver, who was later to throw English Derby winner John Silver.

'The Champion' had proved to be suited to the White City so in early December Conlon sent the dog for another couple of 525-yard opens.

He won the first in 29.16 seconds and the second in 29.02 seconds. This was an amazing run for the time of the year. Monalee returned to White City for the 1966 Longcross Cup, winning his heat by 16 lengths in 30.17 seconds. 'The Champ' not only won the final, killing off the jinx that had followed him thus far, but he took 11 spots off Fearless Mac's six-year-old track record, putting three lengths between himself and runner-up Tric Trac in the process. Five months later Monalee Champion returned to White City to claim the 1967 English Derby. The final was Monalee's first race for Vicki Holloway, Frank Conlon having been obliged to surrender his license due to problems with his kennels.

Monalee Champion, having been made the winter ante-post favourite for the Derby, was given a lay-off during the spring. He was next seen in the Gold Collar, but he was always uncomfortable with the tight Catford circuit. He reached the final without winning a round. His supporters still made him favourite for the decider but he could manage only the runner-up spot behind Stylish Lad.

It seemed that tactics had gone wrong when Monalee went out of the Derby in the first round. He started favourite for the Welsh Derby final after clocking the fastest qualifier, but again he disappointed, finishing last in the field. He ran third in the Select Stakes and third in Wembley's Summer Cup, but it was clear the world had seen the best of Monalee as a racer and he was retired in November 1967. At the insistence of the great Jack Mullan, Fred Warrell purchased the dog for £750. He joined Mullan's Newry kennel and his first pups were whelped in June 1968.

Among the pups born within that first month were Derby finalist Moordyke Champion and St Leger runner-up Moordyke Monalee. A month later Mic Mac, Sole Aim and Cobbler drew their first breath.

Monalee Champion threw the winners of everything worth winning, which included the English Derby (eight finalists), Irish Derby (three winners, nine finalists), and the Coursing Derby. He became the first dog in two decades to sire two American National Champions, Some Prairie and All-Star Bobby. Monalee was reckoned by American breeding expert Gary Guccione to be the best imported sire of dams in a quarter of a century. He sired five All Americans including Share Profit, who was in America's top five sires list for two years in succession, and threw the great American champion and 'Flashy Sir Award' winner, Profits Andy.

Monalee fathered over 1,000 litters in more than a decade at stud. He was blind when he died three months short of his fourteenth birthday. His offspring bred on and still play a massive part in modern bloodlines. Monalee was himself classically bred. His sire Crazy Parachute, who ran third in the 1959 English Derby, is the only dog ever to throw four runners in the same English Derby Final (1967). He fathered seven finalists in total. His only Derby winner was Tric Trac, but other Classic successes included a Scurry (Salthill Sand), a Laurels (Ambiguous), a Gold Collar (Shane's Rocket), a St Leger (Forward King), two Grand Nationals (I'm Crazy, Two Aces) and three Oaks (Majone, Solerina, Shady Parachute). Crazy Parachute also sired TV Trophy winner Spectre II, who became the best sire of stayers of his day with two St Leger winners.

Monalee's dam Sheila At Last would have been barely less famous had she

1969 Greyhound Cesarewitch (from left) Mr F.Taylor (managing Director, West Ham Stadium), Mr. W.G.Warren, owner of Cal's Pick, kennel maid with Cal's Pick, Mrs. W.G.Warren and trainer Jack Harvey.

not produced her 'Champion'. Overall, her Crazy Parachute litter was probably not her best, certainly not on track achievements. Monalee Champion's siblings included Monalee Swallow, who joined her brother in the April Stakes final. Swallow also ran third in Easter Cup and Guinness 575 finals. Another sister, Autumn Rainbow, ran in an Enniscorthy Grand Prize Final, and Monalee Prince was a decent open race stayer. The Sheila At Last dam charts show just how the family bred on though with Waltham Abbey and Ardfert Sean, two notable descendants. In the early 1990s, Monalee's sire line was principally being carried on through his grandson Daley's Gold.

The dog that started at West Ham in 1966 has populated racing with a cavalcade of top quality animals. As such his is a legacy of continuing quality.

One fast bitch

The last Cesarewitch of the 1960s was won by Mr W. Warren's fawn and white bitch, Cal's Pick. Throughout her racing career she was trained at Wembley by Jack Harvey, who saw her as a difficult animal to train. Her time of 32.98 seconds made her the fastest winning bitch ever. Her time was only bettered by two greyhounds up to the disappearance of West Ham – Mile Bush Pride and Prairie Flash. Following her 18 wins and 9 seconds from 36 races, Cal's Pick was to be chosen 'Greyhound of the Year' for 1969 having won nearly £3,000 in twelve months.

By Any Harm out of Flying Sherry, Cal's Pick was bought by Mr Warren for £1,400 at Hackney auction sales; she contested the 1968 Irish Puppy Derby at Harold's Cross. She won her heats and semi-final, entering the final as even-money favourite. However, she was pipped at the post by Always Keen, who was trained by Ger McKenna. Despite this result Cal's Pick was made ante-post favourite to win the 1969 Derby, but a long lay-off, the result of lameness, wasn't the best preparation and she was put out of the event in the early heats.

Cal's Pick was fit again for Wembley's Steward's Cup, and she showed her class by taking the title with a final time of 28.88 seconds. This was followed by her exceptional performance in the Cesarewitch, becoming the first bitch to break 33 seconds for the course and the event. She won each of her heats and in her semi-final eliminated Shady Begonia.

The Prince of Jumpers

The new West Ham track records established in 1970 show Sherry's Prince as holding the 550-yard hurdles time of 30.89. Whelped in April 1967, this brindled dog was by Mad Era out of Nevasca. His owner was Mrs Joyce Matthews and before 1971 he was trained by John Sherlin at West Ham. Alongside Juvenile Classic, Sherry's Prince can probably be said to be the best and certainly the most consistent jumper in the history of greyhound hurdling in Britain. Strangely, he competed in the final flat race to be held at New Cross on 3 April 1969.

In his last race, in May 1972, 'The Prince' won his third successive Grand National. The Grand National is the premiere hurdles event and alongside the Oakes and the Greyhound Derby is one of Britain's senior greyhound Classics, the initial contest being held at London's White City in 1927, the year the track opened for greyhound racing. In its years at White City the National was organised over a course of 525 yards and was always the first Classic of the year. It had been intended to run the National at Harringay but for the greater part of its history it was run at the GRA's oldest track until it was transferred to Hall Green in 1985, where it was set over a 475m course.

In three years Sherry's Prince had 105 outings; he was victorious on 70 occasions and runner-up 15 times. Over the jumps he set new track records wherever he competed. His 29.81 seconds over 525 yards at Wembley in October 1969 was to stand forever, and at Harringay a time of 29.02 seconds for the 525-yard hurdles made him a world record holder, a record he was to break again.

In April 1970 Sherry's Prince won the Long Hop Hurdles at the White City and then contested the Grand National, reaching the finishing post of the final unbeaten. Not long after this, in the Scottish Grand National, he broke a hock,

Over the jumps
Practice for hurdling

Sherry's Prince

SHERRY'S PRINCE		April 1967 brindled dog
Mad Era	Hi There	Stanley Record Dublin Red
	Drumloch Sheevaun	Mad Tanist Sheevaun
Nevasca	The Grand Canal	Champion Prince The Grand Duchess
	Shangri	Keep Moving Hopalong Olly

but still finished as runner-up. It looked as if his career had come to an untimely end, but in October he was back running and in the first weeks of 1971 he won the New Year Hurdles at Wembley and again lined up for the Grand National. 'The Prince' won heat, semi-final and final, taking the title in 29.22 seconds, at the same time equalling Juvenile Classic's two Grand National wins.

Next was the Gold Cup at Wembley. Here, once more, he set a new world record of 28.83 seconds. He took the Long Hop Hurdles again and in January 1972, by eight lengths, he won the Cobb Marathon Hurdles at Catford, run over 810 yards, leaving Adamstown Valley in his wake whilst establishing yet another record. At this point Sherry's Prince was laid low with a kidney infection and once more he seemed to be looking retirement in the face, but in less than two months his excellent powers of recovery allowed him to enter his third Grand National. He took his third title with another unblemished record, which gave him a unique hat-trick.

After his first Grand National win, Sherry's Prince was trained and kept at White City by Colin West who, with kennel girl Irene McNally, nurtured the master hurdler's talents. West trained four Grand National winners in the six years from 1971 to 1976, an unmatched record. 'The Prince' died in 1978 at the age of eleven. Between April 1971 and April 1972 he ran 43 times, almost once a week; he won 33 races and was runner-up five times.

Oh let's hear it for Bradshaw, noble Hammer so fine,
Her battles with the Miller will be remembered through time,
Shout hooray for that glorious West Ham bitch,
That has made every cockney in pride so rich.

Oh sing out for Bradshaw, East London's her home,
She's a runner, a racer and West Ham's very own,
She's brave, she's a champion, she's worth her weight in gold,
Our Coronation Stakes girl, our Jewel, our Bradshaw Fold.

From *'The Ballad of the West Ham Dogs'*

8

AND THEN THE DOGS WERE GONE

Brave Queen entered the Oaks she did,
And like lightning she ran the race,
Never did she balk or skid,
And in victory ended the chase.
So let us praise wise Stan Biss,
The best trainer we've ever seen,
And blow our champion a kiss,
That West Ham dog Brave Queen.
From 'The Ballad of the West Ham Dogs'

The 1971 Cesarewitch, the last to be run at West Ham, was won by Whisper Billy at 50-1, the biggest outsider in the history of the event. Owned by Lady Houston-Boswell, the dog was trained by Charlie Coyle. Whisper Billy was followed in by the 33-1 Rosemount Gunner. This was believed to be the longest odds for a win and place in the history of track racing. The favourite, Dolores Rocket (winner of the Derby and the St Leger), broke down and was retired for breeding. Ironically, Coyle was also to become the last trainer of a White City Derby winner when Whisper Wishes won the 1984 Classic just two months before the west London track closed.

The 1972 Cesarewitch was transferred to Belle Vue, the first time a Classic had been run in the north.

The final days

As far back as the 1950s, when it was more popularly known as Custom House Stadium, there were rumblings that the days of the home of the West Ham greyhound track were numbered, and as such it was something of an achievement that racing continued into the early 1970s. But in December 1971 the owners of Custom House stadium, the GRA (who had taken over the stadium in 1967) made it known that the arena had been sold to a property developer for £475,000.

The Stratford Express, early in May 1972, under the headline 'Bulldozer Men in at Track' reported:

West Ham Stadium, the Mecca of greyhound and speedway racing in the East End for almost fifty years, is to close this month.

The site, which has the largest racing circuit in Britain, is to be used in a redevelopment scheme for 395 houses.

The Stadium will stage its last meeting on May 26 when greyhound racing fans will be treated to a 'gala night'.

The disappearance of West Ham Stadium is expected to bring a big boost to the crowds at Walthamstow greyhound and Hackney Speedway meetings.

The Stadium owners, The Greyhound Racing Association Property Trust Ltd, announced their intention to sell the stadium last July and detailed plans for the site's redevelopment have now been drawn up.

The developers, Budge Brothers & Co. Ltd, intend to build 359 houses and flats on the stadium site ...

The closure also threatens the future of the newly created resident speedway team, the West Ham Bombers, who have been at the stadium since the start of the season ...

The stadium was opened in 1928 and became one of the best known greyhound venues in London.

Only during the war period did racing stop at the stadium, but in 1946 meetings were again held in the arena.

Speedway meetings and more recently stock car and banger racing, became increasingly popular attractions as the stadium fought against fierce competition from newly-built racing stadiums.

About 30 resident staff will be affected by the closure.

Greyhound meetings will continue on Wednesday and Friday evenings until May 26.

An auction of equipment will be held at the stadium on June 6.

The expected positive impact on Walthamstow and Hackney never really happened. It seems that the GRA didn't understand the loyalty that existed for the stadium, its dogs, trainers and speedway team. This kind of support does not transfer easily. The thinking that it should or might is akin to thinking if West Ham United Football Club disappeared that its support would just simply shift to Arsenal or Tottenham Hotspur. To anyone who has been a supporter or fan of any sporting club attached to a locality or area this is, of course, utter nonsense. There never would be another 'West Ham dogs'. This tradition was destroyed by ambition and greed, the type of forces that have no room for the sentiment and care involved in the practice of everyday support.

The redevelopment was part of a whole strategy wherein the GRA looked to take advantage of the rise in the cost of land, which occurred in the early 1970s. The company effectively became an organization concerned with property speculation. This was the start of a chequered period in the history of the GRA. Revaluation of the large areas of land owned by the company situated in many of Britain's largest industrial cities took place, and the GRA began to devote itself to the idea of redeveloping certain tracks as shops and flats. The result was that famous tracks like West Ham and Clapton were closed.

There had been some rumours that the stadium would be rejuvenated; other informal reports hinted that a new arena would be developed on the Custom House site or elsewhere in the Docklands area. However, the land on which West Ham Stadium had been built had a history of subsidence and the location was never well connected in terms of public transport. This, together with crowd and noise pollution in what was an urban area, made the idea of building a new stadium on the site unattractive.

Custom House Stadium hosted a final greyhound meeting on 26 May 1972. West Ham's well-loved stadium, with its dogs, speedway and stock cars, had its own unique atmosphere. There was something about its huge, sprawling acres and its outpost nature, set as it was on the very edge of London's vast metropolis in its abandoned dock area, that had the feel of a no-man's land. The stadium was a principality of its own, with its own peculiar codes and ways of being. It was seedy with a touch of homeliness, ramshackle yet set out on a grand scale. The place had seen better days, but as it gave in to nature it became part of its environment. The whole edifice was a monument to the symbiosis that can take place between an environment and architecture. It is such a melding that attracts people to a place and makes it 'theirs'.

West Ham was one of a number of tracks to suffer from the demise of the sport that was never helped by the popular media. Though greyhound racing was Britain's second most popular sport, scant attention has been given to it by television and radio. For the most part local newspapers ignored West Ham dogs. It was not until 1970 that the first regular broadcasts of greyhound racing were made by Radio London. Neil Martin, then editor of the *Greyhound Magazine*, hosted a special programme devoted to the sport. This was later to become a nightly 'spot', put out at 6.15 p.m. It covered news items relating to greyhounds and selections for the night's racing on the London tracks.

The Treasury didn't help much either, although in 1971 the Betting and Lotteries Act of 1934 was again amended. The change in the legislation allowed tracks to retain more of their income and permitted the tracks to hold 130 meetings a year instead of two each week. However, it was too little, too late as far as West Ham was concerned and a massive opportunity to enhance local sporting traditions had been lost.

In March 1972 the GRA took over Wimbledon Stadium, several of whose directors joined the GRA board. The GRA, having renamed itself the GRA Property Trust, had officially committed itself to becoming a company concerned with land profiteering/speculation. There were fears that if this would threaten the finest tracks in London and the provinces, that they would be lost to the sport. Then, with great suddenness, the bottom fell out of the

Cheerio Everybody until Next Season !!

Come and see me during the Winter.

Do not forget that my kennel friends and I will be Racing every

MONDAY and WEDNESDAY

this month

OCTOBER 28th   NOVEMBER 9th

Great £1,000 Cesarewitch

Last classic of the year.

"London's Winter Racing Centre"

Goodbye West Ham.

property market, the shares of all property companies plummeted, and the GRA Property Trust found itself in grave financial difficulties. But, again, this happened too late to save West Ham.

In Custom House on Tuesday 13 June 1972 the weather was fine. This was unusual as it always seemed to rain on Tuesdays in the docklands, speedway day at the West Ham Stadium. However there was no speedway there on that Tuesday. There were no greyhounds either. Some stadium officials were about, there was also an auctioneer and some businessmen looking for a bargain or two among the fixtures and fittings that went under the hammer that day, the traps, the finishing post and so on. The bits and pieces of the stadium's life were carried away, and after the last bid was made and buyers and sellers had gone home, only the shell of a memory remained.

Millions had passed through the turnstiles and gates of the now forsaken edifice. As the mid-summer evening drew on and the warm darkness began to shroud the terraces, a light breeze ushered the past gently back into the amphitheater. The buzz of crowd, the light bark and whimper of waiting greyhounds whispered for a moment and then was gone. For the first time in the best part of half-a-century the stadium was truly empty and silent. Only the shadows of forgotten memories sighed around the barren bends and sad straights where so many dreams had been realised and many more dashed.

Work on the demolition of Custom House stadium began in October and the bulldozers moved in. The wake of an integral part of a community's cultural heritage was conducted by gangs of workmen tearing down a massive part of the material fibre of East London's sporting history. The famous old arena that had given so much pleasure and joy to so many people of all ages over generations had, by 1973, completely disappeared. Within a few years the whole site was covered by the housing estate that now occupies the space where the stadium once stood. There are roads named after the great speedway riders, but no one thought to have a Bradshaw Fold Street, or a Queen of Suir Road. There is no Appleton Close or Biss Avenue. Greatly loved, timeless and respected names go uncelebrated and without memorial in the area. The first bend of the West Ham track was, by the mid-1970s, just a small green patch at the back of Wilkinson Road.

But the spirit of West Ham greyhounds endures in the minds of those who were there and those that have read this book. As such the dogs have never really disappeared, and they race on in the stadium of the collective mind and memory of all those whose hearts began to beat a little faster as the hare started its run, and who felt their soul jump as the traps sprung open.

Obituary

Six years after West Ham ceased operation forty-eight tracks were operating under NGRC rules, just over 6.5 million people attended 5,847 meetings and tote investment had risen to £70 million. By 1978, attendance had fallen by another half-million from 157 less meetings that ran 45,752 races. The figures continued to deteriorate. In 1980, 5,484,781 people went to the dogs and 20 years after West Ham saw its last race the numbers were down to 5,350,000. However, in Britain, greyhound racing remained the second most widely patronized sport; at this point the six most popular spectator sports were attended as follows:

Association football	25,000,000
Greyhound racing	5,350,000
Horse racing	3,500,000
Rugby football	1,500,000
Cricket	1,250,000
Motor and stock car racing	1,000,000

Greyhound racing has endured despite all the abuse, misuse and poor management it has been subjected to. Governmental greed and poor judgement together with corporate shortsightedness intoxicated with the 'fast-buck' syndrome have battered the sport, and part of the toll was the disappearance of West Ham, with all the hopes and affection it embodied. However, there has never been much room in greyhound racing for apologies, regrets or recriminations. What is important is the next race, maybe at the new 'East End' track at Romford or the posher local choice Walthamstow, or Wimbledon or Oxford, Sheffield, Florida, New South Wales ... anywhere on God's earth ... GOOYON THE SIX DOG!

> Stanley Biss is a trainer of wisdom so bright,
> As the maker of bitches he gets it right,
> He watches and thinks and sees things others would miss,
> This is our man, West Ham's Stanley Biss.
>
> Track master, greyhound teacher sublime,
> He knows every dog, their form he will prime,
> And when the right moment for victory is come,
> A Stanley Biss dog will have the race won.

From 'The Ballad of the West Ham Dogs'

APPENDIX

The Cesarewitch at West Ham 1928-71

YEAR	GREYHOUND	TIME (SECS)
1928	DICK'S SON	32.38
1929	FIVE OF HEARTS	34.82
1930	MICK THE MILLER	34.11
1931	FUTURE CUTLET	34.03
1932	FUTURE CUTLET	34.11
1933	ELSELL	34.22
1934	BRILLIANT BOB	33.80
1935	GRAND FLIGHT II	33.97
1936*	ATAXY	31.24
1937	JESMOND CUTLET	34.56
1938	BALLYJOKER	34.02
1939-44	NOT RUN	
1945*	HURRY KITTY	31.26
1946*	COLNEL SKOOKUM	31.28
1947*	RED TAN	31.30
1948*	LOCAL INTERPRIZE	30.88
1949*	DRUMGOON BOY	30.53
1950*	QUARE CUSTOMER	30.80
1951	PRIONSA LUATH	33.77
1952	SHAGGY SWANK	34.03
1953	MAGOURNA REJECT	33.24
1954	MATCHLOCK	33.03
1955	GULF OF DARIEN	32.99
1956	COMING CHAMPION	33.02
1957	SCOUTBUSH	33.05
1958	PIGALLE WONDER RYLANE PLEASURE	33.06
1959	MILE BUSH PRIDE	32.66
1960	ROSTOWN GENIUS	33.29
1961	PRAIRIE FLASH	32.91
1962	DROMIN GLORY	32.97
1963	JEHU II	33.15
1964	CLIFDEN ORBIT	33.08

1965	LUCKY MONFORTE	33.00
1966	ROSTOWN VICTOR	34.06
1967	SILVER HOPE	32.99
1968	DEEN VALLEY	33.29
1969	CAL'S PICK	32.98
1970	GLENEAGELS COMEDY	33.25
1971	WHISPER BILLY	32.96

* run over 550 yds; all others until 1972 run over 600 yds

West Ham Track Records (1960)

Cock's Sandhills	1942	400yds	21.91 secs
Wireless Time	1943		
Selsey Cutol	1940	525yds	29.26 secs
Drumgoon Boy	1949	550yds	30.53 secs
Juvenile Classic	1940	550yds H	31.4 secs
Ataxy	1935	600yds	33.5 seca
Longfellow II	1933	600yds H	34.94 secs
Lilac's Luck	1946	700yds	39.88 secs
Loughnagere	1930	1000yds	61.16 secs

Track Records (1970)

Come on Wonder	550yds	30.17
Sherry's Prince	550yds	20.89
Cal's Pick	600yds	32.72
Park Nightingale	700yds	38.96
Westmood Villa		
Spotted Nice	880 yds	49.35

Winners of the British Waterloo Cup from the time greyhound racing started to the time of the demise of West Ham Greyhound Track.

1922	Guards Brigade
1923	Latto
1924	Cushey Job
1925	Pentonville
1926	Jovial Judge
1927	Golden Seal
1928	White Collar

1929	Golden Surprise
1930	Church Street
1931	Conversation
1932	Ben Tinto
1933	Genial Nobleman
1934	Bryn Truthful
1935	Dee Rock
1936	Hand Grenade
1937	Perambulate
1938	Delightful Devon
1939	Dee Flint
1940	Swinging Light
1941	Swinging Light
1942	Countryman
1943	Dutton Swordfish
1944	Bryn Tritoma
1945	Maesydd Michael
1946	Maesydd Michael
1947	Constable
1948	Noted Sunlight
1949	Life Line
1950	Roving Minstrel
1951	Peter's Poet
1952	Dew Whaler
1953	Holystone Lifelong
1954	Cotton King
1955	Full Pete
1956	Magical Lore
1957	Old Kentucky Minstrel
1958	Holystone Elf
1959	Mutual Friend
1960	Jonquil
1961	Dubedon
1962	Best Champagne
1963	Himalayan Climber
1964	Latin Lover
1965	Nicelya Head
1966	Just Better
1967	Haich B'e
1970	Rodney Magnet
1971	So Clever

1968 and 1969 cancelled because of bad weather